ANY WAY I CAN
Fifty Years in Show Business

By John Gay
with
Jennifer Gay Summers

Anyway I Can: Fifty Years in Show Business
© 2009 John Gay. All Rights Reserved.

All illustrations are copyright of their respective owners, and are also reproduced here in the spirit of publicity. Whilst we have made every effort to acknowledge specific credits whenever possible, we apologize for any omissions, and will undertake every effort to make any appropriate changes in future editions of this book if necessary.

No part of this book may be reproduced in any form or by any means, electronic, mechanical, digital, photocopying or recording, except for the inclusion in a review, without permission in writing from the publisher.

Published in the USA by:
BearManor Media
P O Box 71426
Albany, Georgia 31708
www.bearmanormedia.com

ISBN 1-59393-318-5

Printed in the United States of America.

Book & cover design by Darlene Swanson of Van-garde Imagery, Inc.

FOREWORD

When I was nineteen, I went to a place as familiar as my own skin, a place I had visited in memories so many times around the dinner table that I knew it by heart. The director at the Boothbay Playhouse, the same theater where my mom and dad had met twenty-five years ago, called and offered me a summer internship and I grabbed it without hesitation. I flew to Maine and took a taxi far from the city, deep into the Boothbay Harbor woods. As we turned into the driveway of the Playhouse, my heart skipped a beat and, in that instant, I knew how my mother felt.

In my mind's eye, I could see my father, in the old yellow robe, on a ladder painting the weathered garage door. My mother's mind in mine, her excitement raised in goose bumps on my skin. A featured actress... a summer rehearsing one show in the day, performing a second at night. Anticipation pounded in our nineteen-year old hearts in unison and just why was that handyman on the ladder staring so hard at her as she swung her Barbizon perfect legs out of her parents' car and into the beginning of the rest of her life?

That day was my beginning, too, not as a featured actress, not even close to finding my husband, but my first day in Boothbay Harbor, the town I would call my summer home in years to come. I suppose I needed to relive their romance, to find the true magic that spun around the three of us kids at the dinner table as Dad recounted the playhouse days he and Mom had courted, when he had acted as leading man to her leading lady, really kissing his lovely ingénue with all the passion an actor could give. Years sweetly remembered as the best years of their lives before television and film gave them their fate.

As my brother and sister and I grew up, names like David Niven, Rod Steiger, Candice Bergen, and Liza Minnelli were a side dish to our roast beef and potatoes. We always enjoyed a lively dining room, our loud laughter punctuated by Broadway musicals or Hollywood film scores.

Years after those dinners ended, I knew it was time to go back again, to revisit the memories that shaped our lives and share them with others. And thanks to Dad's daily journals that went back as far as 1963, he and I were able to remember and record all those times that held our family spellbound at the dinner table, times that are now a rich history of a screenwriter's life. His celebrated scripts have become my family's and Hollywood's fortunate bounty.

Jennifer Gay Summers
August 2008

For Bobbie
and for my children,
Jennifer, Larry, and Lizann

PROLOGUE

It's a bright spring day in 1946, but I'm not in a bright spring mood. A fellow starving actor, Bill Mortensen, and I enter the crowded New York production office on West 45th Street desperate for a job. We join a long line with other hopefuls who are armed with resumes and photos. I have only one photo and no resume, as I've just graduated from the American Academy of Dramatic Arts. I turn to Bill, wondering if we might as well leave. Just then someone calls out from an open doorway. A tall man with a dark moustache is looking directly at me.

"You there. Are you waiting for someone?"

"Me? No, I just...."

"When you're through over there, I'd like to see you in my office."

"I'm through!"

We sit opposite each other at a desk in a small room where he informs me that he's written a play. He's a playwright! He introduces himself as Dick Nash (later known as N. Richard Nash, author of the play and film, *The Rainmaker*). Within moments, he utters the magic words that every actor dreams of. "I think there's a part in it for you. In fact, I think you'd be just right for it. It's going to star the great Broadway actress, Ruth Chatterton."

I try to remain calm, wondering, "Did he just say what I thought he said?" I somehow summon my voice. "Just...uhhh...what is the part?"

"An intriguing role. Challenging for an actor. It's the part of a young fellow with an engaging personality."

I can no longer hide my excitement. Engaging? My God, he chose me from a room full of actors.

He explains that the play is about William Shakespeare in his home at the village of Stratford on Avon. "Every one in town knows a young man by the name of Ben. He amuses them. Makes them laugh. It's not a large part, only four lines."

I wonder how engaging I can be with only four lines.

He proceeds to elaborate. "One of the reasons Ben is well-known in Stratford is his handicap."

"Handicap?"

"Yes, Ben is rather dimwitted, you see, and being dimwitted, he's the butt of many jokes among the peasants. A sort of village bumpkin."

My mind is reeling. A bumpkin? He's being evasive. No...he wants me to play the village idiot. And then I have a second, more disturbing thought. He chose me. He picked me out of a crowd and chose me to play an idiot?

Mr. Nash isn't finished. "He has another handicap."

I wait.

He's looking right at me now as he says, "Harelip. Ben has a harelip."

Before the information can really sink in, Mr. Nash comes up with the crucial question.

"Can you do a harelip?"

I'm stunned. He's describing what some might call a harelip moron. He had looked across the crowded casting office and chose me from all the others. He's waiting for an answer.

It's a decisive moment I can't avoid. I answer his question without hesitation. "Yeath! I can do a harelip."

Mr. Nash is sold immediately.

I leave his office on a cloud, a peculiar kind of cloud. Bill's waiting for me.

"Did you get a part?"

"Ahhh, yes." I move toward the door. He blocks my exit.

"In a Broadway play?" I move on.

"Yes. In a Broadway play."

"Terrific! "What's the part?"

Still moving I say, "One of the villagers. It's a small part but very engaging."

Two days later, Mr. Nash informs me that I have to be approved by the star of the play. Ruth Chatterton lives in a penthouse on the top floor of the Ritz Towers, Park Avenue. A butler opens the door for Mr. Nash and me, inviting us in. Ms. Chatterton is seated at a desk, far across a huge room filled with antique furniture. She looks so imposing, so much bigger than life, that my mouth goes dry. Gazing at me for a long moment, she asks me to step forward. I do as instructed. When I reach her desk, she continues to look me over for another moment. Then....

"Perfect. He's perfect."

STAGE BOUND

CHAPTER 1

Something came into my living room when I was a child and stole my imagination. It took me off to visit places of excitement I hadn't dreamed of. It was called radio and it cost no more than the price of the cheapest crystal set. *Witch's Tale, Inner-Sanctum,* and *Lights Out,* then on to the local movie theaters for fifteen cents on a Saturday morning (a penny for the candy). Flash Gordon in space or Tom Mix on horseback. Those were Saturdays in which I would become a spaceman or a cowboy for the rest of the day. For two bits in the evening, there were feature films like *Treasure Island.* I knew, of course, that Long John Silver was really an actor named Wallace Beery. What a wonderful thing, I thought, to be someone else on screen. To be an actor. Could I ever do that? Of course I could. That was going to be my life. An actor!

With the great depression seizing the country, my parents drove from Wisconsin to Southern California in a battered old Ford. Quite an adventurous move at the time. My brother, Jim, in tow, they first settled in Whittier where I was born. Christened John Thomas Gay, I was immediately nicknamed Jack. Moving several times to various neighborhoods around Los Angeles, Jim and I always shared a bedroom. We were three years apart in age and a world apart in our common interests. Jim was a pragmatist. I was a dreamer.

Dad sold life insurance policies for Prudential that cost twenty-five cents a week. He collected the quarters himself and sometimes he'd take me along with him. I always waited in the car on the streets outside, my eyes on open doorways, hoping they'd pay him. However, these were not the poverty stricken streets of Dicken's London, as I had plenty of open fields to play baseball and football, trees to climb, and dirt lots to create makeshift miniature golf courses with hollowed out tin cans and stolen golf balls.

I dread to think of it now, but a half dozen of us kids would go down a drainage tunnel beneath the street and come out by the Los Angeles River. We shared a dark secret. It was said the old guy who ran the penny candy store down the block had a wooden leg. One day we had the courage to ask him it if was true. We held our breath in fearful silence. He looked as though he might kill us. Then a wild smile suddenly lit up his face. He dropped his pants. The leg was wood.

Three beach amusement parks dotted the Southern California shoreline offering roller coasters, a huge funhouse with slides, and spinning turntables. They were exciting, but not as hair-raising as the major earthquake that hit us in 1934. The family was at dinner and we ran outside, only to discover the bricks of the chimney falling around us. The aftershocks persisted all night long.

I earned some pocket change delivering *Liberty* magazines (a nickel) on my brother's bike, dodging the neighborhood bully who loved to knock me off the bike. Eventually, I was able to scrape up enough money to attend a drama class at the Norton School of Allied Arts in Huntington Park. It was a nine mile bike ride along Manchester Boulevard, past the Goodyear Blimp tied down in an open empty field. At Norton, I started on a road I never left, thanks to my dramatic monologue about a boy out cutting lawns for a nickel with his dog.

"Spot! Come on, boy!" No answer. "Spot!" Up and down the street, he keeps calling. "Spot!"

In a panic, having searched the neighborhood for an hour, he runs off to the dog pound and, out of breath, describes his dog to the clerk.

"He's brown and white, mostly white. Name's Spot, he.... What? You have him? Oh, boy! I'll take him right now! What? Two dollars? Two dollars to get him back? Oh. I'll get it! Believe me!"

The boy returns two days later with the money in nickels and dimes.

"I'm here for Spot!" A dreadful pause. "What? What did you say? ...But No. It <u>can't</u> be too late. You see, he's... He's brown and white, and he's got this spot on his back and... Huh? Oh, no, please. Please! Don't you see? He's my... He's..."

I had no knowledge then of method acting. I didn't know it existed. Performing this at school, I simply <u>was</u> that little boy. The tears came naturally. Not only mine, but those watching me. That's when I really felt it. For myself. The power of being someone else. No question. I was going to be an actor.

Mom took me to an audition for a David O. Selznick production of *The Adventures of Tom Sawyer*. After I read, I felt really good. I felt I had it. They didn't. "Needs freckles." I didn't get the part. Still, I had auditioned for Tom Sawyer.

By this time, Dad's future looked a little brighter. He sold real estate at a new housing development by the burgeoning L.A. Airport. It was called Del Aire, a rip off name from the Beverly Hills Bel Air. The houses sold for three thousand bucks with a hundred down. I attended Inglewood High which was entirely white. Today, it's predominately black. As far as I knew, at that time, there were no Irish neighborhoods, no Polish neighborhoods, no Jewish neighborhoods, and no Italian neighborhoods. Watts was the center of the African American community. With a lack of any ethnic differences, I grew up blissfully ignorant of different prejudices.

Looking back, I realize how fortunate I was with my high school teachers. Diminutive Mrs. Scofield introduced us to Swift and Defoe and Dickens. I never imagined that one day I'd be adapting *A Tale of Two Cities* for the screen with an illustrious British cast. Assigned to write the "what I did last summer" type essays, I took the opportunity to create short fictional stories which Mrs. Scofield felt were grammatically weak. But after dramatizing them aloud before the class, she'd sometimes overlook the grammar.

Mr. Roberts, in history, offered similar chances to speak before the class. I gave a fervent reading of Patrick Henry's address, ending with a dramatic flourish, "Are we to be bound by the price of chains and slavery? Forbid it Almighty God! I know not what course others may take; but as for me, give me liberty or give me death!" What was the date of Patrick Henry's address? I've long since forgotten. But I'll never forget the passion of the speech.

Our senior class play was *Abie's Irish Rose.* I was cast as the Jewish boy, Abie, who falls in love with a Catholic girl. The actress playing the girl was Jewish, which was a switch in ethnicity for both of us. My major shortcoming, as Abie, was a belated and embarrassing voice change marked by frequent tonal fluctuations.

The local theater in Inglewood was called the Academy. On certain evenings, a tower above the theater proclaimed PREVIEW TONIGHT which could be seen for many miles. Hollywood was going to Inglewood for an average reaction from a working class audience. And what previews they were. At *Rebecca*, I saw Alfred Hitchcock in the lobby after the screening. At *Our Town,* William Holden looking over the audience reaction cards. One night, the preview was sold out, and I waited outside for over an hour just to see who the people were in the lobby.

In my teenage celebrity quest one day, a high school buddy and I drove to Sunset Boulevard in my run-down Hudson Terraplane, crossed the center grassy strip on Sunset which ran for miles to accommodate horseback riding, and parked near the Beverly Hills Hotel. In our best Sunday clothes, we entered the hotel and headed for the swimming pool where we had been told we might see them. And we did. One. Right in front of our eyes. Judy Garland. Wet!

By the time I entered Los Angeles City College, my voice was no longer fluctuating and I grew a couple more inches, stretching to six-two. In addition to a liberal arts course, I boned up on my typing from high school and took shorthand, skills necessary for a starving actor. The future would be what I made of it. But, the future had something else in store.

The Japanese bombed Pearl Harbor. It wasn't long before some Asian students on the campus wore metal pins that said I AM CHINESE. As for Japanese families, they were taken to camps in northern California along with their families. In fact, I could see Japanese families being boarded on special buses along Lincoln Boulevard on Thursday mornings. I knew that many had truck farms with produce ready for the market and were forced to give up their homes, their farms, everything. It really puzzled me. They didn't bomb Pearl Harbor. They were farmers. It didn't make any sense.

That summer, Jim joined the army and I, at eighteen, signed up for the draft while working at Bullocks department store downtown. A stock boy in women's sportswear, I worked for Mrs. Pindeck, a very short, stout lady, who was in charge. All employees were required to wear hats to work. Not caps. Hats. I forgot my hat one early morning and circled the stores around Bullocks for an hour to buy one. Nothing was open. Mr. Ramarez, ramrod with steel wool for a beard, was the store supervisor and stood waiting at the entry. I was petrified. He stared at my hatless head. "If you ever come to work at Bullocks again without your hat, that will be your last day."

Before that could happen, a college friend suggested that we fill out civil service exams for a government job until we were called up for the draft. Anything to leave Bullocks. The typing and shorthand skills I had learned paid off. I passed the junior stenographer exam and, to my surprise, was sent to Coast Guard Headquarters in Washington D.C. Routed through New York City on a Greyhound bus, I stayed overnight at the 34th Street YMCA amidst hundreds of servicemen who had flooded Manhattan. For the first time, amidst towering skyscrapers, I felt the pulse of war. Also for the first time, I had the opportunity to go to a theater and see a Broadway play, *Arsenic and Old Lace*. It starred Boris Karloff whom I had known on the screen only as Frankenstein. Here he was in the flesh, live theater. I was enraptured.

CHAPTER 2

Washington D.C. was consumed by war activity, and Coast Guard Headquarters was located in the hot, steamy heart of it. The U.S. Coast Guard Commander Jewell, my boss, was charged with inducting all United States civilian harbor boat captains into the Coast Guard. I rented a small room nearby in an attached row of houses. My landlord was glued to his radio everyday, listening to the epic Battle of Stalingrad where the Russians finally stopped Hitler's troops.

Without any friends in Washington, the weekends were lonely. I came upon a community theater in town that was holding auditions and leaped at the chance for a part. They cast me as a "Negro handyman". Yes, they wanted me in blackface. I still feel embarrassed and disturbed about it today, but at least I didn't play into the cliché of a dimwitted subservient. So far, a Jewish groom and a blackface handyman. But I was on stage.

After eight months at Coast Guard Headquarters, Commander Jewell surprised me one day, asking if I'd like to enlist and continue working with him. He would see to it that I would become an ensign in the Coast Guard. But there was just one problem. The Coast Guard had a far more stringent physical exam than the other armed services. I was scrawny, nearsighted, and my teeth needed work. Commander Jewell said that it would be all right. He'd give me a waiver to be placed in a category called Class "S".

The physical exam took two hours and, of course, they discovered I was underweight, myopic, and my teeth needed work. Commander Jewell gave me the waiver, and I took the oath immediately.

He allowed me to go home for ten days before being officially assigned to his office and suggested I wear a temporary Coast Guard seaman's uniform on the train trip home. The day before leaving, it happened.

I slipped on the ice running for the street car and fell on my left arm. It didn't seem bad at the time. Seated on my suitcase between rail cars, I finally got home, in uniform, and my mother was appalled. My arm was swollen and it hurt like hell. The X-ray showed a fracture. If I had lifted my arm above the vertical, it would have been a compound fracture.

The California Coast Guard medics delayed my return to Washington, and I resumed a romantic relationship with Pat Lesher, a girl who had been in the cast of A*bie's Irish Rose*. We spent quite a few evenings together with my left arm in a sling. In spite of that handicap, it was enough for us to decide that we were definitely in love, but any thoughts of life together at this point would have to wait. My arm healed and my leave was up.

Back to Washington Coast Guard Headquarters, up to the sixth floor and down the hall to Commander Jewell's office. Something didn't look right. There was another name on the door. I soon discovered that Jewell had been sent to duty at sea, leaving no instructions for me. No one knew why and his replacement had no idea what to do with me. They resolved the situation by sending me off to boot camp. No ensign. No Coast Guard Headquarters. Just another lonely recruit arriving at the Coast Guard Station in Sheepshead Bay next to Coney Island.

My platoon was made up entirely of young men from Hartford, Connecticut, who couldn't figure out how a Californian was put in with them. It was so complicated, I didn't bother telling them. The platoon roster read John Gay and that was the name they barked out at roll call every morning. After a few days of this, the guys started calling me John. I stopped correcting them and Jack slowly disappeared.

The station brought me into constant contact with a certain word I hadn't heard that much of before. Every object or situation had the same description. The "fuckin'" food. The "fuckin'" cold, the "fuckin'" drill. The "fuckin'" everything. I came to realize quickly what a sheltered life I had led.

4 a.m. drills, rowing lifeboats through ice flows off Coney Island waters, guard duty, and K.P. became routine. My K.P., however, wasn't in the kitchen. Instead, I repaired heavy canvas floor mats for the gymnasium by lying on my back with the mat propped above me on two sawhorses. Someone lying on his stomach above shoved back a huge thick needle and thread down to me. This activity was supervised at times by the world heavyweight champion, Jack Dempsey, inducted into the Coast Guard and in charge of our physical education. He'd make a brief observation which was always followed by, "Good job, boys!" There was no weekend liberty in boot camp, but we had Dick Stabile and his band on weekends and a new comedian also inducted into the Coast Guard, Sid Caesar.

Four weeks later, word came that the personnel office needed a clerk who could type 60 words a minute. I took the test with three other guys from boot camp. The Yeoman giving the test couldn't believe my score. In fact, he made me take it again to make certain there had been no mistake at 120 words a minute. No more boot camp. I was immediately assigned to personnel. The odd thing about it is I never told anyone in personnel that I had also clerked at Coast Guard Headquarters in Washington D.C. I felt as though it would sound like boasting.

Weekend liberties in New York City. Going to the theater! I wrote letters to the family and Pat and recorded messages for them at the Times Square serviceman's booth. There was Frank Sinatra on stage at the Paramount, Danny Kaye on stage at the Roxy, and the big bands everywhere. Best of all, however, were the stage plays which became my introduction to actors I'd never heard of in plays I loved. Paul Robeson, Helen Hayes, Katherine Cornell, Ethel Barrymore. Magic.

Everything was looking up until a "Dear John" letter arrived from California. Only it was addressed, "Dear Jack". Pat had found someone else. She was going to get married. It was a jolt, no question. But then it made me wonder. Was it all just a high school romance? Shouldn't I be more depressed, disconsolate, angry? I only knew one thing for certain. It was over.

Four Coast Guard buddies and I bunked in the same wooden bungalow on the station. When the commissary served bad pork, we all got violently sick together. A toothache would bring you to the Merchant Marine Base next door where a dental trainee once drilled my tooth without the proper use of Novocain, an experience which is not easily forgotten. We hung out together off base at local Sheepshead Bay bars drinking beer (my first), plus trips to Manhattan where we flirted with girls in Central Park.

One night, a date was lined up with three girls from Albany. We took in a cabaret show at the Hotel Roosevelt on Seventh Avenue where the pianist sang off color songs like, "How I love to nibble-nibble on those cupcakes. Those lovely cupcakes." After the show, we sneaked the girls into a room, moving swiftly past a house detective stationed on the floor. My two buddies got the twin beds while I drew the cot. As it turned out, I had a premature. Devastating. After all, it was my first.

Almost two years of duty and the Special "S" class of my enlistment tripped me up. Men in personnel were being sent to sea and replaced by women in uniform called SPARS, an acronym for the Coast Guard motto, Semper Paratus Always Ready. I tried to get assigned to a liberty ship with my four buddies, but word came back. No sea duty for those in Class "S".

More SPARS arrived at the station. And still more. The Coast Guard didn't know what the hell to do with those in Class "S". Since we couldn't be sent to sea, they came up with a solution which solved their situation. All men in Class "S" designation would be given an honorable medical discharge. The order came down so quickly, so abruptly, I was in uniform one day and civilian clothes the next. In spite of the swiftness of it, however, there was no question as to what I would do now.

CHAPTER 3

Within a month, I auditioned at the American Academy of Dramatic Arts in Manhattan for their fall class before the secretary of the school, Mr. Diestel. An austere man in a pinstripe suit with discolored Roquefort teeth, he sat quietly with no comment when I finished. I was relieved to find out the next day that I had been accepted. Without the GI Veterans Bill of free tuition and fifty-two bucks a month while attending school, I wouldn't have been able to afford it.

To help my finances before school began, I took a job as a page at NBC radio studios in Rockefeller Center. I was back in uniform again, lining up for inspection before ushering for the evening radio programs. It was the time at NBC of the Milton Berle, Perry Como, and Henny Youngman radio shows. Youngman offered us five bucks for any joke he could use on the show. Berle upped it to ten bucks for a joke, but never used one.

Some programs had visiting stars every week, and one of my assignments was to stay with them in the green room until they were due on stage. I found myself in conversations with movie stars of my childhood. There, one night, was Wallace Beery, whom I would never forget as the roughshod Long John Silver of *Treasure Island*. Should I mention that he once inspired me to be an actor? No. I was too timid to bring it up.

On Sunday afternoons, at four, in studio 8H, the NBC Symphony Orchestra performed under the direction of the great conductor, Arturo Toscanini. One Sunday, another celebrated conductor, Eugene Ormandy, substituted for Toscanini and, at the last minute, needed a pair of cuff links. Pages were required to wear them. I eagerly offered mine. Then, I watched Ormandy lead the NBC Symphony Orchestra with my cufflinks, my musical claim to fame. I wanted to get them back, but he kept them.

On another Sunday, with Toscanini conducting, the doors had just closed and the concert started when a short, disheveled man came rushing out of an elevator on the eighth floor lobby. I could see immediately that it was Oscar Levant, the pianist, acerbic wit, and popular entertainer of the time. I rose quickly to stop him. No one was allowed to enter the studio once the doors had closed. He made it clear he was Oscar Levant and he fully intended to go in. I held firm and called my supervisor who arrived moments later. With apologies, he escorted Levant up to the clients' soundproof booth. I thought there might be a reprimand later, but there wasn't. I had acted as a loyal NBC employee. On another encounter, however, I came close to being fired.

Stationed at the entry doors of *The Amazing Dunninger Show*, I watched dazzled as Dunninger performed mysterious feats of mind reading. People were asked to write their names and messages on cards, and he would tell them what they had written without the cards ever leaving their hands. I could never figure out how he did it. It was said that even the great magician, Houdini, couldn't fathom how he accomplished it.

One night after the show, I was stationed at the lobby desk and Dunninger stepped past me toward the elevators. At the same moment, a call came in for him and I summoned him just as he reached the elevator.

"Who is it?" he asked.

With a pleasant smile, I said, "Don't you know?" Understand that I was only nineteen, not really a smart ass, but given to occasional audacity. After all, he did seem to have a way of knowing things.

Dunninger grabbed the phone from my hand, took the call, hung up within seconds, and swept off to the elevator. The next morning, I was given a dressing down by the manager of the page boys. I think the only reason I wasn't fired was due to the shortage of manpower from the war. But it didn't matter. Only a week later, I quit. It was 1944 and a new chapter in my young life was about to begin.

CHAPTER 4

The American Academy of Dramatic Arts was established in 1884. It now shared space with other institutions in Carnegie Hall, utilizing several classrooms and two small theaters. You could sneak into back hallways onto balconies and watch singers, musicians, and actors rehearse in a wondrous cacophony of sound. The Academy's curriculum included teachers of all the different theater crafts. Body movement was taught by a mannish woman, Sarah Strauss, who informed us that we didn't know how to walk, stand, jump, run, or MOVE. We'd begin by pretending we were rats, dogs, frogs, or birds in movement. At the beginning of each class, she'd ask us to speak a line from a play, any play, with an accompanying gesture. One day, I chose a line from *Tobacco Road*. Raising my arms, I exclaimed, "Go to hell you dried up old clod!" A smart ass again. The class enjoyed it, but Mrs. Strauss was not amused.

Voice lessons came from the plump, melodious Mr. D'Angelo who would instruct us to go to the window, open it, and bellow out vowels using diaphragmatic control. "Boomalay, boomalay, boomalay, boom!" Makeup lessons from Ms. Wright acquainted us with the patterns of facial bones and flesh under makeup, lessons which she claimed would prove indispensable if we hoped for a life in the theater. As for acting, there was Mr. Goodman, quite stocky, yet stately and formidable, with a flask of 'cough medicine' always at hand and an empty smoking pipe on his lips.

"Mr. Gay?" he would ask in centurion tones. "Tell me. In this scene, how were you able to state the time, as you just did, without even a glance first at your watch? A mind reader, Mr. Gay?" In Shakespeare's words, Goodman had a "sharp-toothed unkindness". A character, but I loved the old guy.

Quite a different approach was offered by Philip Loeb, a prominent actor of the Broadway theater. "Don't speak the Goddamn line unless you have some idea of what the hell it means! Lines are not just words printed on a page."

I'd always prepare very thoroughly for Mr. Loeb. If he should stop me and ask me at any moment a question about the character I was playing, I'd better damn well know the answer. Loeb made you think, investigate, observe. A compliment from him was something to be treasured. Loeb left the school later to play in the very popular Molly Goldberg show in the early days of live television. It was then that the House Un-American Activities Committee named him as a communist sympathizer. He denied it, but he was dropped from the show and couldn't get work. Loeb later committed suicide in a New York hotel by taking an overdose of barbiturates. Another victim of a vicious time, the "Red Scare".

Mrs. Park, in her eighties, lived near the school on 57th St. She gave me Shakespeare and for the first time made the words come alive. She had toured the country with Southern and Marlowe, a famous Shakespearian company, and knew every female part as well as Hamlet, Richard III, and Macbeth. I would have loved to have seen her on stage.

My favorite teacher was Robert "Bobby" Bell. He had an enthusiastic, encouraging, crackling voice, and he made you feel as though there was genuine talent within you. Apply yourself, work hard, and the world could be yours one day. Some faith in yourself wouldn't hurt either.

All of the staff inspired me on different levels except for one, Charles Jehlinger, head of the Academy. He taught by fear. It didn't work for me. I couldn't help but feel, however, a sense of awe and admiration for this man so small in physical stature. You knew that he knew more about acting than anyone else. His commanding voice would continuously admonish us to "be". Not to "act". To "be" human beings, not actors. His favorite criticism, spoken in a deafening shout was, "You're acting! You're acting!" A great insult.

While embracing a girl in a love scene one day, I patted her on the back. "Stop!" he screamed. "What the devil are you doing? Burping a baby? She's not a puppy dog! She's your lover! Idiot!" Anyone who attended the American Academy in those days has a story about "Jelly". It was said that he reduced Spencer Tracy to tears and Edward G. Robinson to fury. They all respected him because they knew he was right. I can still hear those words. "You're acting! Acting!"

There were two young women in my class from Oklahoma. Irene Champlin was looking for something new and different after her husband, a pilot, had been killed in the war. Annabelle Roberts, Irene's best friend, had a heavy Oklahoma accent and no real hope or desire to be an actress. She came along with Irene for the fun of it. They shared a large apartment in Tudor City by the East River which I visited on many occasions for company and food and rehearsing and food and empathy and food. Pals we were, that's all, joined by another student, Jim Carr, who later skipped the senior class and went on to become a Broadway producer along with his step brother, Robert Fryer.

I was rooming with a classmate now, Joe Gorman, on upper Broadway. We shared a small studio room and took the subway to the Academy everyday, but Joe never reached the senior year. Instead, he got a part in a Broadway musical, *Dark of the Moon,* which any one of us would have preferred to another year at the Academy. Having lost my roommate, I moved in with three other classmates to a cold water railroad apartment (long and narrow) on 57th Street. We all shared a large front room of the apartment and one bath down the hall. Within easy walking distance of the Academy, the place was sublet to us by an elderly couple who had comfortable living quarters in the rear. We were told the husband was a disbarred dentist from Arizona, but we never found out why.

Junior class graduation plays finished the semester in a theater in the basement of Carnegie Hall. I was cast with a stunning statuesque brunette, Armina Elvander, who happened to be the niece of Lawrence Langer, a founder of the most prestigious producing company on Broadway, the Theater Guild. The play was *The Shining Hour*, by Keith Winters, and the part called for me to play the piano on stage. The only way it could be accomplished was by having one of my classmates, a classic pianist (but a lousy actor), play a backstage piano and look through a window on the set so he could see my hands on stage every moment while I pretended to play. The illusion worked even better than we had hoped. Armina and I were husband and wife in the play. A femme fatale enters the scene and the husband falls for her. I remember the woman playing this part mostly for the unexpected deep insertion of her tongue during an onstage kiss.

At the time, the *Theater Guild on the Air* was a popular radio show (later to be televised). Armina invited me on occasion to drive to the studio with her in her uncle's limousine. One time, I was even given a crowd line in the play *Abe Lincoln in Illinois*. The radio announcer made a terrible mistake that night in promoting the following week's show. It was scheduled for Ray Milland who had won an Academy Award for *The Lost Weekend,* but a substitution had been made at the last minute. "Next week," said the announcer, "the leading part will be played by that Academy Award winner, Sonny Tufts." Tufts was well-known, very handsome, but a less than respected actor who had never won anything. Reactions from the announcement went from puzzled to incredulous. SONNY TUFTS? It then became a byword for any under-gifted actor. Poor Mr. Tufts.

Only one hurdle left in my junior year. An invitation to return for the senior term in the fall. I got it, but I was now faced with two simmering hot summer months that stretched before me in Manhattan with no job in sight. Irene Champlin, thank God, came to the rescue. She knew a summer stock producer, Sherwood (Sherm) Keith, who was in town looking for actors and apprentices for his playhouse in Maine. I auditioned and was taken on as an apprentice with room and board. Good enough for me.

CHAPTER 5

The Boothbay Playhouse was buried in the woods, just a few miles from the rockbound coast. It was a resident stock company with the same compliment of actors all season. I arrived by train at a small rail station in Wiscasset with another apprentice, Lloyd Roux. Sherm picked us up in his 1936 Ford woody station wagon and drove us to the theater. Built to look like a barn, it was the reverse of genuine barns being transformed into theaters. We had barely put our belongings away in the large old clapboard house next door when Sherm put us to work digging post holes by the road to support a sign which said "Boothbay Playhouse 500 Yards Ahead". To me, however, it said Emerald City and I might as well have been transported to The Land of Oz. The house had only one bathroom with two public ones in the theater. The company took showers outdoors behind a guest bungalow with designated people on lookout to insure privacy.

The theater, closed since the beginning of the war, desperately needed publicity. Sherm brought in well-known models, cover girls from Powers and Conover agencies, all of whom hoped to become actresses. In fact, a leading publication that year, *Look* magazine, called it the Cover Girl Playhouse. Dorian Leigh was a well-known model in the fashion world at that time, her picture having appeared on many *Vogue* magazine covers. She starred in the very first production, *Blithe Spirit*. As an actress, Dorian was a beautiful model. It seemed that beauty ran in her family as her kid sister, Susie Parker, had become an internationally famous model and socialite. I was appointed stage manager for the production and helped to build the set. It was not my last experience with *Blithe Spirit*.

John Goss, a teacher at the Rhode Island School of Design, became our set designer and arrived with his wife, Ethel, who was somewhat jealous of his time away from her when he worked at the theater. A friendly, talented man given to wearing salmon and apple green trousers, John became quite a father figure to me in succeeding years at Boothbay. Another lovely model was Jackie McGowan who used the professional name of Adrian Storms. Some sparks flew between us that summer, but nothing really developed. I was so completely dedicated to the theater that I didn't want to get involved with anyone. Imagine. Twenty-one years old with a stock company of attractive young women and all I wanted to do was to get on stage. Dedication or insanity?

With a schedule of ten plays, Boothbay introduced me to a way of reading plays that I had never known before. Only one complete mimeographed script was sent each week to a summer stock company. Along with it were distributed "sides" for each part which contained only the cues and lines for that part. The director cast from the master script, assigned parts, and it wasn't until the first reading, with everyone present, that the actors knew what the hell the play was all about. A so-called black side with many lines was obviously a lead part. It was an economical way of distribution for the publishing companies with no regard for actors. All scripts and sides were returned at the conclusion of each show.

With only three very small parts that year, my sides were anything but black. I assembled sets, tore down sets, painted flats, and borrowed furniture and props from local people in neighboring towns. Busy all summer but, for me, it was over far too soon. However...the American Academy would be there in the fall and what could be better than that?

CHAPTER 6

Manhattan and no place to live. I checked into a seedy hotel on 45th and Broadway. On my first morning, in the bathroom across the hall from my room, a huge rat dropped from the ceiling into the sink before me. I ran back to my room and called the desk clerk in the lobby. Minutes later, I heard someone singing in the hall outside. I opened the door to reveal the drunken hotel manager, still singing and swinging the rat, alive, by the tail. "Caught the sonofabitch!"

The next day I left the hotel and persuaded the disbarred dentist to let me come back. Only a small room was available now in the 57th Street railroad apartment. Small doesn't do it justice. Berle or Youngman would have called it a casket without handles. One thing for certain. It beat rats dropping from the ceiling.

In my junior and senior years at the Academy, there was a vivacious young woman from Mississippi with a delicious Southern accent, Joan DeWeese. By far, she was the best actress in the class which impressed the hell out of me. A romantic interest, no question, but… there was also an unexpected call from Jackie McGowan, the cover girl model from the Boothbay Playhouse. And what about Armina Elvander? She was back for the senior class and invited me one wintry night to a party in Greenwich Village held at the large brownstone home where she lived with her uncle, Lawrence Langner. It was a gathering of actors, directors, and writers with Burl Ives performing at the piano. I was in a world that I had always dreamed of. And, I couldn't take my eyes off Armina. Could she be the one? Before I left, there was a long, lingering embrace and kiss at the doorway.

However... Jackie McGowan had asked me to stop by her apartment that night, just a few blocks away. I hadn't seen her since Boothbay and it was only eleven o'clock. She met me in the downstairs vestibule where things got unexpectedly warm very quickly. With a glance toward the street, she told me her husband (a husband?) was seeking a divorce and might have someone watching her apartment. Perhaps, we'd better meet another night. I readily agreed, left her in the vestibule, and walked out to see a man standing across the street. Who? I didn't stick around to find out.

The next morning at school, I rehearsed a love scene with Joan. Long golden hair, classic high cheek bones, a slender figure, and not the least, a talented actress. We worked together so well. Joan? Or was I in love with Armina? What about Jackie? It's hard to believe, I know, but sex was not a part of it. Not yet, at least. It was a time of innocence far different from today. I was in love with...romance.

A goodbye call to Jackie. No 'husbands' for me. And Armina? She expected an amorous pursuit after that party at her house. Instead, I had Joan in my arms on stage. Things continued that way for a few days and then got worse. Joan was convinced I'd fallen in love with Armina and avoided me. Here was the fodder of Shakespeare's comedies. I was hung on my own petard. Looking back today, I can't help thinking what a delightful winter that was.

Spring graduating plays were held at the Bijou Theater, right off Broadway on West 45th Street. *Life with Father* was playing there at the time and the Victorian drawing room set was used, no matter what the play. It prompted some very tricky staging. Joan and I had the leads in *Blithe Spirit* and I say, without any modesty, although years younger, I was a hell of a lot better than the guy who played the lead in Boothbay. Romance with Joan cooled off. We both hoped that an agent might see us in the play and call, but there were no calls. Couldn't they recognize talent or could it be that we were far too young to be playing sophisticated English socialites?

Bad news from home. My parents were getting a divorce. I had no hint of any problems between them. But Dad had met someone else. Under the circumstances, my sympathy went to my mother. Correspondence with Dad eventually stopped. A wall grew between us. My fault. I should have tried harder.

CHAPTER 7

The time had arrived. We, graduates of the American Academy of Dramatic Arts, were out on our own where the odds were stacked against us. A world of struggling actors, but we chose it and we got it. Making the rounds of casting agents was a task of monumental endurance and ego-busting rejections while we traipsed from one office to another in the Broadway area. It was always thus as it is today. My rounds were made somewhat less discouraging with the cheerful companionship of Bill Mortensen, my friend from the American Academy. His wife made marvelous spaghetti marinara, piled high, and that became my only real meal of substance every two weeks. I'd have to say youth got me through. Not to mention blind determination.

It was at this time I reached the production office of the play *Second Best Bed*, by Richard Nash, and I became Harelip Ben. An "engaging" part? Well, for me, it was the opportunity of joining Actors Equity. In fact, it was more important than that. It was the affirmation of a boyhood dream. I was now going to become a professional actor.

Second Best Bed was derived from words in Shakespeare's will in which he wrote, "I gie unto my wife my second best bed." The implication was the first bed was for his mistress. Ruth Chatterton would play Shakespeare's wife, Anne Hathaway, while rehearsals would be under the direction of both Chatterton and Nash. As it turned out, she did most of the direction. Ms.

Chatterton's husband, Barry Thompson, and her ex-husband, Ralph Forbes, were both in the cast with very little friction between them. After three weeks of rehearsals, Ms. Chatterton started calling me "Baby Ben".

We opened first in Schenectady, New York, to fair reviews, then Toronto to excellent reviews, and then to Chicago, fair to good reviews. Also assigned to the position of assistant stage manager, I checked the set each night to be certain everything was in place, calling the curtain time for the actors and "holding script" in the wings during a performance ready to prompt the actors should they go up, forgetting a line.

One night in Chicago when Ralph Forbes did go up, I repeated the line. And repeated it. Nothing. The stage manager in the opposite wings gave him the line from her position. Nothing. Finally, Chatterton ad-libbed a line or two that brought him back on track. As the curtain fell, Forbes was furious, shouting at me, "You never gave me the line!" He was ready to fire me. Chatterton quickly made it clear to him that she not only heard the line, but that anyone in the back of the balcony could hear the Goddamn line!

I kept my job, but from that time on, Forbes never liked me. On stage playing Harelip Ben, I accidentally tripped on a step and the audience laughed. Forbes accused me of doing it on purpose. "Don't you ever try that again!"

"Yes, Mr. Forbes. "I'll watch my step, Mr. Forbes."

Ruth Chatterton, however, was always kind, gracious, encouraging, with a lilting voice that I loved. She had a habit of wearing nothing beneath her Elizabethan gowns and when I knocked at her dressing room door, she startled me when, sometimes, her gown was accidentally at half-mast.

"Five minutes, Miss Chatterton."

Opening night on Broadway. Only a month out of drama school. A telegram came to the theater for me from Jehlinger himself. "We are all sending you our sincerest wishes for a successful beginning." I stood on the stage alone checking the props. I thought of the kid who loved *Treasure Island* and was determined to be an actor. Of the boy who told a story of losing his dog, Spot, amidst tears. Tonight it was only four lines with a nasal accent, but I was on Broadway.

Twenty minutes before curtain, Ms. Chatterton suddenly appeared on the set. She'd never come out onto the stage like this, early, before the curtain. She was calm, reflective.

"This," she told me, "is the good part. The work. We'll do our best. Some critics out there will like us and some, I can promise you, won't like us. In fact, they will come with knives ready to strike. Don't be afraid, Baby Ben. It comes with the work. You want a life in the theater?"

"Yes, Ms. Chatterton."

"Be prepared."

The curtain went up. The applause lasted well over a minute. I timed it. I was thrilled and I thought she was, too. She hadn't appeared on Broadway in a number of years, and it was their way of welcoming her back.

The next morning was black Thursday. The reviews weren't bad. They were devastating. "*Second Best Bed* Is No Bargain," said one headline. Some reviews were downright vitriolic. "*Second Best Bed* Is Not So Good." And "Annie Shouldn't Live Here." Even though they were charitable to Ms. Chatterton, she was crushed as she had so believed in the play. And for my review as Harelip Ben? There was only one. "We do not forget the simpleton either." What a sendoff.

We continued for seven more performances before closing. It was goodbye to the cast and, as it turned out, I never worked with any of them again. But I would always remember Chatterton's words that first night in New York before the curtain. Life in the theater. Be prepared. Well, let me have it, I thought. I'll take it anyway I can.

CHAPTER 8

Another hot summer in New York loomed, but Sherm asked me back, thank God, for a second season at the Boothbay Playhouse. He'd already formed a resident company and I was the last one signed. It was an altogether different company than the year before. A smaller one without cover girl models, but it turned out to be a greater opportunity. I was given three featured parts and appeared in *The Importance of Being Earnest* which we performed with white and black costumes on a white and black set. The play introduced me for the first time to Oscar Wilde. His wit and dexterity made such an impression on me that it became extremely important in my life years later. Once again, the summer went by far too quickly.

My hole-in-the-wall room on 57th Street was available again, and I was off to the endless round of theatrical offices. The Walgreen's drugstore at the Hotel Astor was an actors' haven. A few hundred square feet of coffee counter and camaraderie for actors as broke as you. One would never approach a friend at Walgreen's and ask, "What's new?" Meaning, "Are you working?" God, no. In the first place, if your friend had found a part in a play, you wouldn't have to ask. It would be forthcoming immediately. Over coffee, we studied our Bible, the weekly casting sheet. Everyone was looking for a part that everyone else was looking for. Any part.

I continued to visit Joan DeWeese in her studio apartment which had a narrow balcony overlooking 57th Street. Her roommate was Gaynelle Nixon, a buoyant, attractive young actress who struck gold that year in a Broadway play. I would soon become fast friends with "Nixie" for life. Their apartment was a refuge from my cold water digs. Joan and Nixie supplemented my weekly fare, a loaf of bread and a jar of peanut butter, with coffee and cinnamon toast. Occasionally, I'd take a temporary typing job, never telling my employer I was an actor. You couldn't if you hoped to be hired. Actors are here today, gone tomorrow, and not to be trusted. There were times I hocked my high school Royal portable typewriter at a nearby shop on Amsterdam Avenue, but never for much money as I always wanted to be able to get it back.

Mom invited me to come back home for a few weeks. She had rented a small commercial building on South Vermont Avenue in Los Angeles where she ran a garment business making dresses for wholesalers downtown. She had four women helping her from their homes while she specialized in the stitching and machines at her shop. With her instruction, I attempted the buttonholes task myself, but seemed to misplace the holes every time.

The old building she leased had a separate large room in the front section which she was able to sublease for a tidy sum. The people occupying it immediately installed several telephones. It soon became obvious they were bookies. The county sheriff's office was only two blocks away, and one had to assume they knew what was going on. Mom managed quite easily to ignore it.

A small nightclub on the corner across the street had members of a four piece jazz band. They'd visit her often in the evening between sets, a place to get away from the club for awhile and relax. She'd hear their problems, sympathize, and play a little poker.

With a library nearby and only city college behind me, I felt an overwhelming need to fill in some blank areas of my education. I became a dedicated and indefatigable student of my own curriculum. Already familiar with many of the great playwrights, I moved on to the celebrated writers of fiction, non-fiction, to the works of famous painters until I could tell the difference, at least, between a Monet and a Manet. It was a strange period living in a little room in the back of a dress factory, pouring over books. A period in limbo. I was anxious to return to the theater.

CHAPTER 9

My third summer at the Playhouse required the usual mundane chores before the season began. One morning, while painting a garage door on a ladder in my ragged old yellow terry cloth robe, a car appeared in the driveway. Out of it stepped a knockout blonde ingénue, Barbara Meyer. Her parents had driven her up from New Jersey to be certain it was a safe environment for their daughter. Having already seen her black and white publicity photo hung on a wagon wheel in the lobby, I eagerly awaited her arrival. She glanced briefly at me and assumed I was a maintenance worker. It wasn't until later in the day when our eyes met that she recognized me from the American Academy. A graduate from the class after mine, she had seen me there, but I hadn't been aware of her. I certainly was now. Even her publicity photo didn't do her justice. But could Barbara Meyer act?

Our first play together was a comedy called *Petticoat Fever* written by Mark Reed, a very successful playwright, who had a summer home nearby. Mark came to the show opening night and there were very few laughs. After the curtain came down and the audience had left, Mark stepped up to the proscenium and offered a lesson in acting that would always remain with me. "You're pushing for laughs. Play it straight. Relax. Play it real. The laughter will come." And then he offered the classic advice which today has become a mantra for actors. "Less is more."

The next night proved him right, of course. The laughter was continuous. I discovered that a summer stock experience could be just as valuable as the time spent in a classroom at the American Academy where Jelly's voice shouted, "You're acting!" I also discovered the answer to my first question. Barbara Meyer could act.

Sherm assigned me the part of Sheridan Whiteside in *The Man Who Came to Dinner,* an outrageous character with the opening line of "I may vomit". I was on stage every moment with only a week's preparation. My device was to memorize the lines first without any rehearsal or any thought of characterization. When I had the lines down pat, and only when I had them down, I'd then dig into the character without having any worry about the mechanics of the lines. It was the very opposite of method acting, of course, but it worked for me. It had to. There was no time. Playing young or old, "less is more" was never forgotten.

Before the summer was over, Barbara became Bobbie and we played leads in *Arsenic and Old Lace*, the same play I had seen on my New York stopover trip to Coast Guard Headquarters. We clicked. Both onstage and off. But something felt quite different this time. I wasn't going to lose this romance.

My steadfast coffin room on West 57th Street awaited me, and I soon found a clerk-typing job as well as a part in an Equity Library Theater production of a Molière play to keep me busy. Bobbie and I met at the apartment on East 73rd which she shared with Irene Champlin, my friend from Academy days. Racing across Central Park at night to avoid being mugged, I had no more doubts about Bobbie and she felt the same. Any competition for our hearts would come from the theater.

A friend from Boothbay was working that winter at the Reading Playhouse in Reading, Pennsylvania. He called to ask if I would be willing to work there as a set designer. I had certainly built enough of them in Boothbay but was disappointed this would not include acting. I left a clerk-typing job and took it without hesitation. As it turned out, I did get some offstage lines in the play *Home of the Brave.* I trucked in a ton of dirt for a jungle set and delivered my lines while hidden behind fake painted palm trees. "Yellow Yankee bassard! Come out and fight, Yankee Bassard!" I made a lousy Japanese soldier.

CHAPTER 10

By the time summer rolled around again at the Boothbay Playhouse, Sherm was ready with two summer stock comedies, followed by productions far more fulfilling for both actors and audiences. The opportunity to play leads in George Bernard Shaw's *Pygmalion* and Arthur Miller's *All My Sons* was living a dream. As the anguished son, ashamed of his father for betraying his country in *All My Sons,* the tears came naturally. Six nights, two matinees, and when you're really getting deeply into it, it's gone. In summer stock, you're constantly moving on. No choice. But each experience sure does add to an understanding of the craft.

As for Professor Higgins in Pygmalion? Okay, forget Rex Harrison. Forget Leslie Howard. They don't exist and shouldn't. Think only Higgins. By the time the curtain fell on the last performance, I felt I had come as close to the character as any twenty-two year old actor could on a summer stock schedule. Self-confidence goes a long way.

Most character roles, for me, required white hair. I used a traditional makeup called clown white. By the end of that season, some people in Boothbay audiences thought the John-Bobbie romance was a May-December affair. One night, leaving the theater after the show, I turned to her and made a not so romantic declaration. I said, "When we get married..."

"Get married?"

"Right. Of course."

She didn't appreciate the abrupt quasi-proposal, but she didn't think about it for long either. We made the big decision and put off the date until the following year. That is, after I made a formal request to her father, Ozzie, for his daughter's hand. I'm sure that both Ozzie and Dottie felt uneasy, to put it mildly, that their daughter was marrying an out-of-work actor. Prelude to a most uncertain future. But they never said a word to me. I asked them why once. They said, simply, that they knew I loved her.

CHAPTER 11

Once more that damned beloved 57th Street hole in the wall. Bobbie and I had a different goal this time. We had to earn enough to have some kind of nest egg before a May wedding and return to Boothbay. I was hired by a middle-aged widow, Mrs. Lenart, who had taken over her husband's business, the Lenart Vari-typing Company on West 44th Street in the diamond district. I didn't tell her when applying for the job that I was an actor or I never would have been hired. She had two other women working for her, mimeographing shipping contracts for steamship companies. The small two room office had no air conditioning. Very few places did back then. In fact, a lot of things weren't quite as sanitary as they are now, and certain times of the month were particularly unpleasant. At any rate, typing blue stencils all day was...BORING.

Bobbie had now found a job at the fashionable Bergdorf Goodman store on Fifth Avenue, modeling clothes and avoiding the manager, Uncle Eddy, whose hands were much too handy. She lived for awhile at the Martha Washington Hotel for women. Their strict policy instructed men to sit in the lobby and wait for their young lady friends to meet them downstairs.

When making theatrical rounds, we used the standard published audition material that everyone used. I wanted something different for us and wrote a couple of dramatic monologues. Nothing came of them for me, but

Bobbie got a small part on a television play. And then another. She was a perfect ingénue, but the parts were terrible and I told her so.

Television was in its infancy. Mostly seven to twelve-inch black and white images, with no one knowing quite what to do with this new medium. Maybe I could create a light comedic show for us. Just the two of us. Newlyweds, as we soon would be. I wrote a ten minute audition sketch and we performed it for advertising agencies, showing how we could include a commercial plug for one of their sponsors. One producer, Harvey Marlowe, showed some interest. He said that a new network, WOR-TV, would be going on the air in the fall and he'd try to get them to think about using us. Bobbie and I didn't hold out much hope.

When I told my boss lady I was getting married, she was dismayed. It wasn't that I was getting married to Bobbie. She and the two women in the office had met her and liked her very much. I told them that we were now going off to a summer stock theater in Maine. I said that Bobbie was an actress and I was hired to run the box office. Yes. I lied to them. They offered me the opportunity to stay and become a sales rep for Lenart Vari-Typing. They couldn't believe it when I turned down such a generous proposal. Actually, I would have made a terrible sales rep. I felt guilty for lying as I had come to have a lot of affection for them. But guilty as I was, nothing could take me away from the theater.

To my surprise, the Lenart ladies came to the wedding on Mother's Day, May 7th, 1949, held at a small vine-covered chapel in Plainfield, New Jersey. I was apprehensive that they might find out my "box office" subterfuge from the many friends and relatives there, but they didn't. My mother came in from California, and my brother and his wife drove up from North Carolina where he was a disc jockey on a local station. "Ave Maria" was sung by Bobbie's sister, Jan, who had a glorious, professionally trained voice that would serve her later in several opera companies. Needless to say, the tears flowed.

In the men's room at the reception, one of Ozzie's friends actually came up alongside me at the urinal and asked, "How do you intend to support

Barbara?" It really floored me. Together, Bobbie and I had saved a few hundred dollars. I don't remember what I muttered in response, but I thought the question on this night, on this occasion, at this place, was insensitive. The truth is all of her family's friends were concerned that Bobbie was marrying an actor. The poor girl. God, what a terrible thing to have happened. We left the reception for an inn a few miles away and, although we kept the name secret, someone found out and called us at 2 a.m. to wish us "Happy Mother's Day!"

The Sky Top Lodge, in the Pocono Mountains, was and is a lovely resort with acres of towering trees and trimmed lawns. At the end of a long winding driveway, our car was immediately met by bellhops. When one of them opened the trunk of the car we borrowed from Sherm, the trunk latch suddenly ripped the side of our suitcase. It was a gift from the Lenart ladies, made of reinforced cardboard. I pretended not to notice.

The honeymoon was limited to three days, as Bobbie had been offered a part in a *Kraft Television Theater* production. The first rehearsal was called for 9 a.m., so we left the most beautiful room in this most beautiful resort at 6:30 a.m. and ended up in a traffic jam on the Pulaski Highway. I dropped her off at 9:45 a.m., and she raced in ready to face the consequences. The worst of sins is being late for rehearsal. Especially the first day. We thought it would surely be her last. Instead, she was astonished to find everyone with welcoming smiles. All was forgiven. You don't get an excuse like a honeymoon everyday.

After the show aired, we arrived in Boothbay as a married couple for the first time. Three or four actors from previous years returned that summer, and my mother drove out from California in her Chevy coupe to join the company, helping out with the numerous household chores. The playhouse routine began and we shared leads again, opening in the first play of the season, *For Love or Money*. Then something happened that changed everything.

Harvey Marlowe, the man who saw our audition in New York, called to say WOR, Channel 9, had signed us to do a domestic comedy in the fall. They wanted a fifteen minute show, five nights a week. "Who will write them?" I asked.

"You will."

Fifteen minutes? Five nights a week? All we had was the ten minute audition sketch. Impossible. And I'm not really a writer. I called Harvey Marlowe immediately.

"We're thrilled with the offer."

It was our last year at the Boothbay Playhouse. I'd spent five seasons there and Bobbie three. So many parts in so many plays. Comedy, drama, tragedy. How fortunate we were. Only summer stock could offer such an opportunity to play a gamut of parts before paying audiences. I never thought of it at the time as a prelude to playwriting. Of course not. I was an actor. The writing would just be a diversion.

CHAPTER 12

Winter was upon us and the john in the outside hall of our newly found two room apartment was beyond cold. It froze you to the seat. At twenty-five bucks a month on Perry Street in the Village, we could put up with the potbelly coal stove for heating, the small ice chest dripping water, a bathtub with a lid that served as a kitchen table, and a friendly mouse. We bought a sofa bed, some used furniture, and we painted the place. I started writing feverishly with my old, trusty Royal portable. My first script, *Apartment 3C*, was on its way.

WOR-TV was using the facilities of the shuttered New Amsterdam Theater on 42nd Street, the old home of the *Ziegfeld Follies,* as a television studio. *Apartment 3C* would be the second show for the fledging studio, airing October 11, 1949, with Harvey Marlowe as producer and director. With fingers crossed, we went on the air Monday night and, although we felt pretty good about it, the next morning brought only one review, *The New York Times*. Negative.

Time to bow out? WOR still wanted us and why not? It hadn't cost them anything but three dollars to make our contract legal.

With our savings disappearing, however, it became obvious that we couldn't go on for lack of life support. Informed of this, WOR magnanimously came through with an amount that allowed for three meals a day at the venerable nickel and dime emporium, Horn & Hardart.

A variety of shows were scheduled to follow ours. There was an opera singer, a comedian, musical groups. One horrible act I will never forget. A man had what he claimed to be a talking dog. A dog that could also play the piano. During rehearsal, the dog did strike a few notes of God Bless America, but the talking was something else.

"Hamburger!" the man would say. And the dog would intone, "Um-mmbaaagaaa".

"No!" the man would scream. "Hamburger!" and he'd smack it across the nose. The dog would try it again. And again. Several hard smacks would finally bring something a little more recognizable.

That night on the show, the smacks were replaced by little dog biscuits. Just a sweet loving master with a talented dog. Myself, I was ready to smack the smacker. In fact, I've avoided all circus animal acts ever since then.

The nightly broadcast meant writing the script the night before, memorizing it the next morning, taking the subway to the theater and, with time and space limited, two run-throughs, a dress rehearsal and... Showtime! Five times a week with weekends off to rack the brain for new ideas and scripts.

One morning, the Lenart ladies came around to see us at the Amsterdam Theater. They had been astonished to find John Gay on television with his wife. And we were astonished to see them after all this time. I really didn't know what to say. What the hell. I lied. I'm an actor. They took it well and seemed pleased for both of us. I neglected to tell them that we weren't being paid by WOR as much as Lenart paid me.

As the show progressed, there wasn't much of a chance to get acquainted with our neighbors on Perry Street. The lovely actress next door, Doreen Lang, was appearing with the Lunts in *Oh Mistress Mine*. Her husband, also an actor, watched me come down the stairway one morning with a heavy basket of coal which broke apart and tumbled with a roar down the steps. Ever sedate, ever composed, he smiled, a gentle smile, stepped nimbly around me and moved on.

Shouts across the courtyard in the summertime filled the air.

"Shut your goddamn mouth, bitch!"

"You stinking bastard!"

Our only quiet neighbor was the very small mouse. It would suddenly appear at our sofa bed and rise up on its hind legs, looking at us with a puzzling curiosity before scampering off again.

We were given a feature article, "Tea TV for Two" in a new magazine called *Telecast*. "Light, breezy and sometimes naively ribald, Barbara and John really don't have to reach too far into the recesses of their minds to come up with authentic, straight from the feedbag material…it sure is a nice happy feeling to know that two youngsters can start on nothing and zoom to the top just by being themselves."

The fact is, however, that our fifteen minute script, five times a week, became a formidable task. The domestic problems of a newly married couple with only two in the cast every night were getting repetitious. What to do about the heavy daily schedule? The old saying that dying is easy, comedy is tough proved all too true. What if we changed the format to mystery? What if we added three or four to the cast and made it a half-hour format? To our surprise, WOR was agreeable but <u>only</u> with three or four more. The schedule would be Friday nights fifty-two weeks a year. Life would take on a slightly more normal existence.

WOR moved its TV operation to a spacious studio environment at the ABC Center near Central Park West. They now brazenly called our show *Mr. and Mrs. Mystery*. With just four more in the cast getting minimum payments, there wasn't much of a choice at guessing the villain. It made a daunting challenge for me.

The usual live TV mishaps occurred, of course, but in our case, budget limitations made us prone to them. Many a dead body would rise before the camera was off. It was usually our floor manager who had to get back to his cues. With three run-throughs now and a dress on the day of the broadcast, the actors were inclined to go up with more frequency than they might in a well-rehearsed play. It was necessary for Bobbie and me to learn everyone's lines. I'm proud to say no detected pause lasted longer than five seconds during the show. One night, we were able to persuade Bobbie's father, Ozzie, to play a telephone linesman. Just one line which he forgot, I covered, and he refused to appear again.

In one rehearsal, an actor struck me on the back of the head, as scripted, but it landed with such force that I almost passed out. He repeated it on the second rehearsal and I told him to lighten up. That night during the show, however, I staggered from another heavy blow. Bobbie ad-libbed and we carried on. We never used him again.

One memorable night, I suffered a deep cut on my hand in an opening scene as I picked up a prop diamond made of glass. The cut was deep, and I thought for a few scary moments that I might have severed a major artery. I kept my hand in my pocket the entire scene, trying not to look obvious about it while also trying to hide the crimson tide on my white summer suit. Incidents like that make you grateful for the years you spent onstage prepared to cover any situation.

We were now beginning to see people staring at us in the subways. Could that be? With the recognition, additional money came to us now from advertisers who wanted us to promote their product live just before and after the show. A recorded tune, "Miller - High Life! – Miller High Life! The champagne of bottled beer!" would play as I spoke and it still jangles in my ear to this day. I also had to drink warm Miller beer on camera which would later produce inescapable belching during the action. The sponsor, naturally disturbed at this, decided to place the commercial at the show's conclusion. They offered us no free samples which was a shame because Bobbie and I were already furnishing the union crew two bottles of bourbon at our expense at the end of each week. A little gift expected for their cooperation. Another WOR show, *Twenty Questions*, used us live on their program for commercials extolling the virtues of Ronson cigarette lighters which I always feared would mistakenly come tripping out as "Ronson fiogerette lilters".

Our studio adjoined a much larger studio where a dramatic anthology,

Robert Montgomery Presents, had elaborate, expensive sets next to ours that we longed to use. Our show certainly couldn't afford the top stars they had every week, but we <u>were</u> able to cast many fine actors and actresses in New York at the time. There was one actress, in particular, named in a column by Jack O'Brian in the *New York Journal American,* whom he said was under suspicion by the McCarthy Red Channels group for what they called subversive activity. O'Brian warned us to be careful and not hire any more "red commies" for our show. We had never investigated anyone we hired for the show and employed them based on their talent.

Ignoring the O'Brian warning, we continued to hire actors as we always had. There were no repercussions, but I was interested to see in the 2006 film *Goodnight and Good Luck* that Jack O'Brian was mentioned as the newspaper columnist who attacked a newsman, Don Hollenbeck, for being an Edward R. Murrow supporter, calling him a pinko commie sympathizer. Like Philip Loeb, my teacher at The American Academy of Dramatic Arts, the revelation destroyed Hollenbeck's career. Both men committed suicide.

The time came when we left the coal bucket, the frozen toilet seat, and the subways far behind us and moved to Demarest, New Jersey, just across the George Washington Bridge. We had decided, after all of these years, that city life with all of its metropolitan stress was not for us. We found a gardener's cottage on a large estate owned by Milt Herth of the Milt Herth Trio, a New York cabaret musical group. The cottage came with a vegetable garden that occasionally provided us with food. It also fed a clever little ground hog which our neighbor shot one afternoon. That unfortunate event took away any appetite for our garden vegetables.

The trip to work meant buying a car and driving to the studio at an hour that escaped the daily commuting traffic. By this time, WOR afforded us the luxury of more actors and additional writers. Frank Wayne, whom I had worked with onstage in Boothbay, took over the direction.

On several evenings now, after the show, a call would come at the station for Bobbie. Some distressed person, always a woman, would ask Mrs.

Mystery's advice for a problem she was experiencing with some threatening relative or friend. Bobbie was always very sympathetic, but made it clear the woman should contact the New York Police Department for help. It did give us a jolt to think that there were lost souls out there who believed in Mr. and Mrs. Mystery enough to call us for help. Well...not us, exactly. They always asked for Mrs. Mystery.

After two years, in the fall of '52, word came from on high of our cancellation. Two years was a longer run than we had ever anticipated. We said our good-byes, both on and off the air, and I looked forward to an uncertain future. Acting or writing? Perhaps an income from writing could support us while we looked for jobs in the theater. In a medium so new as television, producers, writers, and directors were on an almost level playing field. Opportunities were certainly there. But I had to have an agent.

CHAPTER 13

A lovely silver-haired widow of a TV executive, Blanche Gaines, was acquiring a stable of young and struggling TV writers such as Frank Gilroy, Rod Serling, and Carey Wilbur. Blanche worked from her apartment at the Park Vendome on 57th Street. Within weeks, she got me a writing assignment on a mystery series for Dumont television. More cops. More guns. The Blanche Gaines writers and significant others were invited to come together at her cocktail parties, and the Gilroys became our closest friends. They remain so today. The Serlings would also figure closely in our lives.

A network variety program called the *Ken Murray Show* included fifteen minute, live on stage, human interest dramatic sketches. The short play I submitted was accepted ($300) and cast with the little known Angela Lansbury and Robert Cummings in the two part play. I was so encouraged that I followed it with a half-hour drama, *The Ferry Boat Crisis at Friday Point*, in which the captain of a ferryboat has his livelihood threatened when his midwestern river town proposes to build a bridge. The captain goes on strike, engendering a crisis.

Blanche Gaines thought it had a chance and sent it to the popular CBS program, *Lux Video Theater*. It was less than a week later that she informed me they were buying it. As if that wasn't heartening enough, Blanche called later to say that Fredric March and his wife, Florence Eldridge, agreed to star in it. Two revered actors of the American theater had signed to do a script of mine. I was thrilled. Thoughts of a future acting began to fade, but refused to disappear. I'd go with the tide for now.

After ten days of rehearsing, March and Eldridge performed live just as they would for the theater. And they were both brilliant. There was only one unavoidable moment at the play's conclusion. Ms. Eldridge, seated at a mock dressing table and turning directly to the TV camera, remarked with dramatic feeling, "I don't know about you, but I always use Lux toilet soap for my skin." It was mandatory for actresses doing the show. Picture Glenn Close at the final moments of a *Hallmark Hall of Fame* having to declare, "I always send a Hallmark card when I care enough to send the very best." It was live TV. It was both wonderful and appalling. It was "The Golden Age".

Lux Video Theater called me to write another show on speculation. They didn't like it and passed. Another. They passed. How long could we keep our garden cottage? Several new television shows were being created on the West Coast. Perhaps there'd be better opportunity there. Maybe a chance at a feature film.

My mother was overjoyed to have us come out. We sold our car for much needed money and put an ad in the paper offering to drive a car to California for anyone who might need the service. A response came within a week. The man had a vague memory of seeing us once on *Mr. and Mrs. Mystery* and trusted us immediately.

Eight days later, we pulled up in front of the small clapboard house in Los Angeles that my mother was renting now and delivered the car. I set to work immediately on my Royal portable typewriter. Bobbie got a job at Coast Federal Savings and joined a car pool on a nearby corner to get to work. We also shared the house with a very large, white, female angora cat that seemed to be in heat all the time, judging from her suitors who arrived daily, circling her and howling. She loved the attention and teased them mercilessly.

In spite of the background music, I wrote a script called *Bilshan and the Thief* which Blanche sold to an independent California producer. She finally sold a two person play I had written before we left the East which starred the Academy Award actress, Louise Rainer. It seemed now that I was committing myself to a possible writing career. Committing is one thing. Making a living at it is another.

Four years of marriage and no children. <u>Not</u> because we didn't try. Medical tests revealed that my low sperm count was responsible. I then endured weekly fertility shots, painful injections in the gluteus maximus which might be more correctly identified as a pain in the ass. In addition, I drank a daily dose of a white milky liquid so vile that I still can't get the taste out of my mouth. I should have been potent enough to populate the population of Los Angeles. No results.

More scripts, no sales. While Bobbie worked at Coast Federal Savings, I fell back on my clerk typing skills once again with a job at Rubbercraft Manufacturing, typing up manifests on the shipping dock. Thank God it was outside the building. The smell of the rubber in the plant was more than I could bear. As with the Lenart ladies, I never disclosed to Rubbercraft that I was an actor or writer.

Bobbie and I continued working, but it was getting increasingly obvious that I was getting nowhere. A return to New York seemed to be in order. Time for another lie. I told my employers at the rubber company that I was going to work for my wife's father in Manhattan. "A big mistake," they said. "Never work for your father-in-law!" I was urged to stay on as a sales representative with a bigger salary. I declined. They even threw in a lifetime supply of condoms which was the <u>last</u> thing in the world I needed. And so we returned to bustling New York City with no baby, no feature film, scrambling for ideas for new scripts.

CHAPTER 14

In the play, *My Sister Eileen* (also a musical, *Wonderful Town*), two sisters live in a basement apartment where they see only the feet and ankles of those passing by on the street above. We found a similar, inexpensive place on King Street in the East Village. Our second night there, the doorbell awakened us at 1 a.m. Two men asked for Harriet. I told them we didn't know her and had just moved in. Two nights later, three others came looking for Harriet again <u>and</u> Shiela. It became evident this time that the women who had last rented our apartment were hookers. Busy hookers at that. By the end of the week, we had to put a little note on the door. PREVIOUS OCCUPANTS HAVE MOVED. The note helped, but it still took quite a while before the nocturnal visits finally ceased.

The place was heated by a kerosene stove which had to be fed by five gallon cans from backbreaking trips up Eighth Avenue, ten blocks away. The weight of the kerosene, compared to the coal on Perry Street, was no improvement. Bobbie found a job working on the executive staff of a modeling agency, Barbizon, just off Fifth Avenue, owned by a woman consistently in an alcoholic haze. I was back on my trusty portable amidst the constant hum of a paper manufacturing plant just down the street. In addition, we had the nocturnal company of giant cockroaches crawling along the baseboards.

Blanche Gaines told me a producer, Paul Monash, needed a writer to help him with a daily kid's show called *Atom Squad*, created in New York and performed live in a broadcast from Philadelphia. One of us would plot the week's scripts and the other write the dialogue. Every other week, we would reverse the process. A kid's show? It was $350 a week and I accepted immediately. It gave me work for six months until the inevitable cancellation arrived.

We were replaced by a comedian named Pinky Lee. He was a baggy pants, pie in the face sort of clown whom the kids loved and Paul hated. "The bastard took away our time slot!" While we tried to create a detective series afterward, Paul would interrupt our work to turn on the TV set and watch Pinky, hoping that he would fall on his ass. He didn't. Our detective series did. It never even got off the ground. But, at least, I didn't have to go on writing lines like, "You'll never get away with it." As for Paul Monash, he went on to become a major TV and motion picture producer.

With the help of an ABC television editor and noted novelist, Charles Jackson, of *Lost Weekend* fame, I was able to sell a thirty minute script to *Armstrong Circle Theater*. No guns. No cops. Having pitched the idea, Jackson advised me to write it as the third act of a stage play. Start on a high dramatic note and never let up. It worked.

The reputable Neighborhood Playhouse School of the Theater offered me the opportunity to write the book for a musical for their graduating students. They offered very little money, but it was the chance to attempt something I had never done before. Among the young cast members at the time were Robert Duval, Suzanne Pleshette, and a young man who later became a director, Sydney Pollack. The school was so pleased that they gave me a bonus and asked permission to use it again the following year.

One morning, in our basement apartment below the street, Bobbie woke up and threw up. Something she ate, no doubt. But she felt lousy all day and threw up again the next morning. My God. Could it possibly be true? Could all of the gook I swallowed and the shots in the ass I suffered have paid off? After six years of waiting, we celebrated by going up to Boothbay Harbor for a summer week with her parents. Bobbie threw up all the way. Fantastic! We were going to have a baby.

I had just finished writing a Civil War play for television, *The Day Before Atlanta*. Knowing we had a baby on the way, Blanche Gaines was thrilled to tell me that Herb Brodkin at ABC, Center Stage Productions, was buying it. I watched two or three rehearsals which I thought flat and unpromising due entirely to a new actor brought out from Hollywood. I asked the director if he could be replaced. But he had a better idea. "Let's get him into a Union soldier's uniform during rehearsals and see what happens." It worked like magic. Lee Marvin became the part.

Another member of the cast, Luther Adler, a legendary stage actor from a family of actors on Broadway and the Yiddish theater, was cast as a ruthless sergeant, Jubal Early, named after a Confederate general. He thought the name, Jubal, sounded like "Jewboy" and wanted it changed. No problem. I came up with another Confederate general, Gant. The climax of the play called for Adler to be killed on a winding stairway with a dramatic fall down the steps. This was live television, however, and the director said he couldn't maneuver the cameras for such a shot. Not on the steps. Adler replied, "I die on the stairway or I don't die at all!" Mr. Adler got his way performing live for the cameras. The reviews were very encouraging.

With Bobbie's expanding waist, we decided once again that city life wasn't for us. We moved to an apartment in Chatham, New Jersey, where our first daughter, Jennifer Lee, was born. I looked at her through the nursery window. Puckered and beet red, she resembled an infant Dwight Eisenhower. Bobbie's mother, Dottie, was standing beside me, enraptured. "Isn't she beautiful?"

Frank Telford, an enterprising producer at the Dumont Network, was starting a half-hour series called *The Stranger* in which the leading character appears at a critical moment to aid victims of injustice and, just as quickly, disappears. More humanity and fewer cops than the usual fare. I wrote every other show for six months all performed live on studio stages. Before the last show was televised, another event came along so unexpected and so tantalizing that I couldn't resist.

Neil McKenzie, whom I knew at the Boothbay Playhouse, was opening a season of summer stock at the Robin Hood Theater in Arden, Delaware. He wanted me for the entire season. On stage again! I may have left acting, but it never left <u>me</u>. The list of plays and parts offered were a magnet. Ephriam in Eugene O'Neill's *Desire Under the Elms*, Kit Carson in Saroyan's *The Time of Your Life*, the lead in Clifford Odets' *The Country Girl,* plus five other productions. This was an Actor's Equity Company with a union protected salary.

Arden is a small residential community of large homes under a canopy of shady trees. A major drawback to going there was the fact that Bobbie and Jennifer would have to remain in Chatham, New Jersey, a two hour drive from Arden, and could only visit me on weekends. I didn't want them to be alone in the apartment, so they moved in with Dottie and Ozzie.

For the play, *The Time of Your Life,* Neil jobbed in an African American for a leading part. It's difficult to believe now, but the actor was barred from the restaurant where the cast usually ate after the show. This was not the Deep South, but Delaware in 1955. Their explanation? "If we serve a Negro, others won't come in." With that, <u>we</u> stopped coming in.

Another actor who arrived for *Three Men on a Horse*, Phil Leeds, was one of the funniest men I've ever known. In fact, it was difficult to act on the same stage with him without breaking up. There was, however, a very serious crisis going on in his life. He was due to be called up the following week before the House Un-American Activities Committee in New York.

It was understood that if he refused to name anyone, his whole livelihood would be in jeopardy. He asked for advice and I told him it was something he simply had to decide for himself. I didn't think he would name anyone, however, and as it turned out, he didn't. True to his expectations, he had no more TV or film work for a long time. A brave, funny, frightened guy.

The role of Ephriam in *Desire Under the Elms* was once played by the Broadway actor and film star, Walter Huston. This was summer stock and we had only the usual one week's preparation. I buried myself in the part day and night and found I was becoming disagreeable to everyone around me at the theater. I didn't care. I was living the grim, angry patriarch, Ephriam. The local critic seemed astonished that we could pull it off in that limited time. He wrote, "A play such as this takes courage to stage it and physical strength to play it. A rich, wonderful experience and I wouldn't have missed it for the world." You don't get a chance at parts like that very often.

CHAPTER 15

Having saved most of my salary that summer, I now faced an uncertain fall, this time with a wife and child. We set up a small living space in the basement of Bobbie's parents' house. I was still thinking of an acting career when a newspaper article about a boy who confronted and befriended a suspected murderer caught my eye as a drama for a television play. I took a line from the scriptures, "Be sober, be watchful: your adversary the devil as a roaring lion walks about, seeking whom he may devour." I turned part of it into the title of my play, *The Devil as a Roaring Lion*, creating a story of such a boy. His moral dilemma was caring for a wounded man whom he believes might be the Devil.

To my surprise and delight, *Kraft Television Theater* on NBC snapped it up quickly. Two fine character actors, E. G. Marshall and James Whitmore, headed the cast directed by George Roy Hill who later went on to direct *Butch Cassidy and the Sundance Kid*, among other great films. The play had very good notices, but during the broadcast, something unanticipated occurred. When the boy was about to speak the line from the scriptures, "the devil as a roaring lion", the very title of the play, he went blank. Forgot the line. People must have wondered where I got the title. Live TV. Truly, nothing like it.

Kraft held a contest that year, inviting the public to choose their favorite production of the year from the fifty-two plays. The winning writer would receive fifty thousand dollars. I came in second. And for that? Zip. They might have taken the fifty thousand from their yearly budget and spread it out with a thousand bucks more for every writer. They might have? Hardly. The Golden Age did not produce much gold. I must say, however, that <u>live</u> television had its upside. It was more akin to theater than to film. Not only were there rehearsals everyday for two weeks, but the writer was often present.

This was a time when certain dramatic programs were starting to broadcast in color. I wrote what I felt was a sensitive, poignant drama, broadcast on NBC, called *Prairie Night* starring Martha Scott. Lacking a color TV set, Bobbie and I watched it in a car dealer's showroom in Greenwich Village who used the novelty of color TV to bring in customers. We looked at the people around us. This time a live audience. I could instantly see their reactions.

The Civil War period had always fascinated me and the idea of two brothers taking opposite sides in the war could present a very strong dramatic conflict just as the country was being torn apart. I used the framework for my story of a Confederate foray into enemy territory on a mission to destroy a Union railroad trestle. I called it *The Sentry.*

NBC's *Goodyear Playhouse* produced the play and skipped the usual scheduled rewrite sessions. No lines, no words would be changed. Sidney Lumet, who later became one of filmdom's finest, was hired to direct, and I found him to be a writer's dream in rehearsals because he enveloped himself in everything: the period, the place, the characters. It was Lumet who wanted to use my preface to the script as a voice-over narration before the play begins.

"There were three of them, and they came by foot.

Their uniforms, although shabby, were definitely the gray and butternut of Hood's Army of the Tennessee. They were tired men...not from the hazardous journey...but hopelessly tired from having lived with death too long. Their mission was doomed from the start, but that was a circumstance impossible to foresee."

It was also Lumet who wanted a sound of crickets outside of the rail station in the opening scene. Easily done, but I told him that historically, the event took place in January. No crickets.

Chapter Fifteen

Arriving in the midst of rehearsing, Lumet would immediately grab me. "Take a look at this! See what they've done with this scene!" Enthusiasm. Dedication. Sydney Lumet.

The play had an excellent cast and the reviews were all that I could have hoped for. "A splendid example of the dramatized idea," from the publication *Best Television Plays 1957*. Later that year, it was published in *Perspectives*, a collection of stories, articles, and plays designed for university students. I hoped then that it was good enough for another assignment. The hope became a reality when *Omnibus*, a respected Sunday show encompassing all of the arts, hired me to write a play about Robert E. Lee at Gettysburg. I turned in an outline. They didn't like it. In fact, they hated it. There we were again, our financial situation reaching a nadir.

We looked for a less expensive place to live in the far reaches of the Jersey countryside. The far, far reaches. We found a stone mill house, dirt cheap, in a dirt farm pasture. With cows. Look out any window and they were there. And just as we were about to make the move, a phone call came from the West Coast.

BIG SCREEN

CHAPTER 16

Three men, Harold Hecht, James Hill, and Burt Lancaster, had seen *The Sentry* on the night of the telecast. They represented the most successful independent film company in Hollywood and their story editor wanted to know if I'd be interested in writing a motion picture for them. If? I tried to remain cool. This was, after all, just a week before we were about to become neighbors with a field of cows. The editor, Bernie Smith, told me they owned a book, *Bandoola*, by J. B. Williams, which they wanted adapted to the screen.

"Would you read it, Mr. Gay?"

With very little hesitation, I said I would. "Bandoola?"

"It's an elephant."

"Oh. I see. An elephant."

"If you wish, we'll send you a copy."

"Uhh...do. Yes. Please do."

"Good! We'll send it right off."

I read every page of it twice. A Burmese boy and his beloved elephant escape from the advancing Japanese in Burma. The premise was provocative, but the plot slowly fell apart, and I couldn't figure out a way of doing it. Never mind. I'd work it out.

"Engrossing," I told them. "Gripping."

"Would you be interested in flying out to California to talk about it at our expense?"

"Let me see. Yes. I think I can manage that."

Three days later, I entered the lobby of the H.H.L. office building on South Canon Drive in Beverly Hills where tropical exotic birds were flying about in a two story cage. I met with Mr. Smith and with fingers crossed and all the enthusiasm I could muster, I told him of a concept I had arduously worked out for adapting the book. It was good enough to get an affirmative response.

"We'll need an outline treatment first. A thousand a week. We'll contact your agent in New York." I was introduced to Hecht, a man even shorter than the dimunitive Bernard Smith and to Jim Hill, handsome, urbane, and engaging. Lancaster offered an amiable smile.

That night, I called Bobbie. "A thousand a week!"

Ten days later, she joined me with Jennifer in California where we rented a modest two bedroom stucco house close enough from H.H.L to walk to work. It meant we wouldn't have to rent a car except on weekends if needed. We had no friends here except the Serlings. Rod had just moved his family out, having signed a contract with MGM. While Bobbie pushed little Jennifer in her stroller along the streets of Beverly Hills, I struggled with *Bandoola* in a small windowless office. The elephant became my savior and my nightmare.

After a month of this, the company told me they were going to New York City to produce a film called *The Sweet Smell of Success*. They wanted me there for *Bandoola* story sessions while they were shooting. Ernest Lehman had written the script of *The Sweet Smell of Success* from his own original story and he was hired to direct. Unfortunately for Ernie, however, Burt Lancaster decided to play the lead. And he now wanted Clifford Odets, the noted author of many plays in New York, to do a rewrite with Sandy MacKendrick directing. As they say, "That's showbiz." It was a devastating blow for Ernie at the time. But he sure as hell didn't let it stop him, as witness *North by Northwest* and many successful films since then writing and directing.

Chapter Sixteen

Back in California, I turned in my treatment of *Bandoola*.

"My God, John, what is this?" came the complaint. "This is a treatment for a Disney film! We don't do Disney films! A boy and his elephant? Pure Disney!"

I reminded them, gently, that *Bandoola* was, indeed, a book about a boy and an elephant. A book <u>they</u> had optioned. To this day, I don't know what else they thought I might do with it. So. Dark Friday. They would let me know Monday what future plans there might be for me, if any. Our California visit was over. Back to the stone mill house and, God forbid, the cows.

CHAPTER 17

Harold called me into his office Monday morning and I was thrown a lifeline. The company had purchased a war story. If I agreed to adapt it for half the salary I'd been making, they would throw in a bonus *if* the script made it to the screen. One last chance. I accepted without a moment's hesitation. Unlike the hapless *Bandoola,* I loved the book, *Run Silent, Run Deep,* written by a former submarine captain, Commander Edward L. Beach. Harold needed the script by a certain date, a rush job, and I soon found myself working seven days a week, morning 'til evening on the screenplay. Bobbie's days became even lonelier.

Script conferences were sometimes held at five in the morning with just Hecht and Hill. It soon dawned on me they wanted to go over the script without Lancaster present. They never told me why. Other times, with just Burt present, I found his suggestions no better or worse then theirs. In fact, Burt put them across in an extremely dynamic and persuasive way, standing in his office before a giant noisy waterfall which flowed over the rear wall. He'd throw his whole body into it, and I was mesmerized by the performance. I'd think to myself, "Yes. That's right!" But when I got back to my office and faced the typewriter, I slowly realized that what he had in mind wouldn't work. I'd been taken in by a charismatic Lancaster performance.

One Saturday night, Bobbie and I were invited to a large party at Lancaster's house in Bel Air. Actors, directors, and producers filled the huge living area, but Lancaster's wife and four kids weren't present. Bobbie, meeting Lancaster for the first time, was dazzled by him like many women. When she was searching for the ladies room, Burt took her hand and guided her upstairs. I could tell she was apprehensive, and I was too, but it turned out there was nothing to be disturbed about. He was an absolute gentleman. The disturbance came later in the evening. I'd already completed three-quarters of my first draft of *Run Silent, Run Deep* and Burt, under the influence of many drinks now, announced to me that the project was commercial crap and we shouldn't be doing it. He made it sound as though it was beneath both of us. I was flabbergasted to say the least. Was this the end of it?

The next morning, a Sunday, I was working at the office when I found myself too disturbed to write anything. I finally picked up the phone and called Harold, telling him that Burt didn't want to do the film. A silence at the other end of the line and then, "I'll take care of this. You keep writing."

Burt called an hour later. He was sorry about last night, he had too much to drink, and he certainly intended to do the picture. I couldn't help but wonder though; would this picture really be made?

Deadline on top of me and only three more pages to go. Harold appeared in my office at one o'clock in the morning so drunk he could barely stand. I couldn't get rid of him. How do you politely say, "You're plastered." Get the hell out if you want this finished!"

Instead, I offered a few gentle words about my concentration being diverted. "You <u>would</u> like it tomorrow?" He looked at me for a long moment, nodded, fell into a chair, and went fast asleep.

Once I had the first draft, Harold brought in a retired admiral to go over the script for authenticity. Having been a lower rung third class petty officer in the Coast Guard, I was intimidated at first, but he turned out to be very helpful, giving me needed confidence on the script.

Along came my second astonishing break in what I now thought could be a screenwriting career. Frederick March and Florence Eldridge were one thing, but this was going to star Clark Gable and Burt Lancaster, both filmdom superstars. Could it be? My first feature film? Could I finally put thoughts of a cow pasture behind me? Topping it all, Robert Wise had agreed to direct. This was before he went on to direct such pictures as *The Sound of Music*, *West Side Story*, and my favorite, *The Sand Pebbles*.

Hecht decided a visit to a submarine in San Diego was now in order. We boarded early, Hecht, Wise, and I, all of us bushed from staying up late the night before. The boat's captain (subs are called boats rather than ships) welcomed us aboard and off we went on scheduled maneuvers with other Navy craft into open sea. They had me sit just behind the chief boatswain at a board of red lights which would all turn green when fully submerged.

"Keep your eye on the center red light," he said. "It's the last light to turn green, indicating the conning tower hatch is secure and we are fully submerged."

I did just as instructed and the shouting began (they always shout), "Dive! Dive! Dive!" With my eyes glued to the lights, I saw them turn from red to green while more commands were shouted. All lights turned green except the center one. Still RED. Did I get it wrong? Should I say anything? Should I tap the boatswain on the shoulder and point it out? Within seconds, however, water started pouring down from the conning tower above us. The ocean was flooding in. More shouts, more commands. It was controlled pandemonium, if such a thing is possible. "Reverse engines! Reverse engines!"

The crew scrambled to surface the sub. A lanyard had caught in the hatch above and was secured. Then "Dive! Dive! Dive!" was heard once again.

Safely submerged, we set out to sea in maneuvers that had to match mock encounters with other Navy craft in which dummy torpedoes would be used. By lunchtime, Wise and I were still bushed from lack of sleep and asked the captain if we could just sack out for twenty minutes. He was glad to oblige and let us use his own quarters with double-tier bunks.

I had only just closed my eyes when the sub gave an alarming shudder, a groan, another shudder, and started to sway back and forth. "Uh-oooga! Uh-oooga!" came on the loudspeaker. And then utter silence. No engine sound.

Wise and I sprang to our feet. Two crew members entered the captain's quarters and the air-tight hatches were sealed behind them immediately. Silence. They stood on guard, still silent, hands behind their backs, at attention.

"What's going on?"

No answer. No response. The silence was both deafening and alarming. They stood there like statues. And they remained that way for what seemed like an hour. Then a voice came over on a loud speaker. "Secure from collision drill! Secure from collision drill!"

A grinning captain greeted us when the hatches were opened. It was obvious that he enjoyed his little stunt enormously, taking Hollywood for a ride. The first shudder was all ahead full to all reverse. Second shudder was firing off a dummy torpedo. How did it feel? We offered weak smiles. "Oh, yes. Terrific stunt. Great."

CHAPTER 18

H.H.L. was riding high and I couldn't help but notice very attractive women in the hallways. Not for casting. At least not for a picture. I was never certain which one of the trio, Burt, Harold, or Jim, was the reason for their visits. Perhaps all three. As the new writer on board, it seemed wise not to inquire.

One foggy morning, Harold chartered a plane to take Wise and me to Catalina where he planned to greet us off Avalon harbor on his yacht. We sat at the Santa Monica Airport with visibility ZERO. Surely, no pilot would go up in this weather. But, a cheerful young man turned up and led us to an amphibious plane. And, as it turned out, we never lost sight of the ocean below because we were never more than thirty feet above it. We hit the water on pontoons under a suddenly sunny sky just a few hundred yards from Harold's hundred and fifty-foot yacht moored in the harbor. I thought to myself, this is it. This is Hollywood.

The next morning, discussing a scene with Wise and Hecht on the ship's fantail, a woman's voice exploded from the cabin below. "What's going on up there you sons-a-bitches! I'm trying to sleep down here!" This was my introduction to Gloria Hecht, Harold's wife. She was extremely irritated by our voices, but I found out later that a state of irritation was her omnipresent condition. We moved our discussion elsewhere.

The first day's shooting on *Run Silent, Run Deep* took place at a house on Ocean Boulevard in Long Beach. There, on the front lawn, stood Clark Gable bigger than life. There was Rhett Butler from *Gone with the Wind* and Mr. Christian from *Mutiny on the Bounty*. A warm handshake, gracious and less flamboyant than Burt. I liked him immediately.

After a week of filming, Burt decided he wanted to go over several scenes with Gable. They were to meet, along with Harold and Jim, at the H.H.L. building on Canon Drive. There was still summer twilight when I arrived and, to my amazement, seated on the concrete steps outside of the building, was Gable with his wife, Kay Spreckles. Gable was more than irritated, "The goddamn door is locked and no one's inside! What kind of a cheap outfit is this?"

Gable had lost his cool and I couldn't blame him. He asked if I had the key. No. Like Gable, I expected Harold to be there. I told them there must be some mistake. Harold would <u>never</u> forget an appointment like this. I raced down Canon Drive to a pay phone on the corner and was told that the appointment had been changed to eight o'clock. Not to my knowledge and certainly not to Gable's. As Harold lived only a few blocks from the office, he arrived within minutes, apologies flowing. Thus we began.

The Navy saw the project as an opportunity to promote the submarine branch and offered technical assistance never before quite equaled. Actual Navy equipment was incorporated onto the set of the sound stage. A periscope assembly was so heavy that the floor of the stage had to be bolstered to hold it up. One-fifth size model submarines were built for the ocean battles while a rear admiral made doubly certain that everything was authentic.

It was well-known by all who ever worked with Gable that he always came in fully prepared knowing every line, as written, and expecting the same from his fellow actors. Unfortunately, the actor playing opposite Gable in the first scene of the film was given to improvising lines. He was replaced the next day by Jack Warden.

We were three weeks into shooting when a very serious problem developed. Gable wanted to make a basic change in the screenplay in which the commander of the boat, Gable, has to make a battle decision that almost sinks the sub. Having lost the crew's trust, he's threatened with mutiny by their leader, Lancaster. It was a scene directly from the book. Gable, however, having flown long range bombers in World War II, said he didn't know of any mutiny on any naval vessels in the war. I had no idea if there were or not, but I did know we were in trouble if we had to stop shooting at $50,000 a day. We stopped.

I don't think Gable ever forgave Harold and Burt for that night when he and Kay sat outside on the steps of H.H.L. on South Canon Drive. It's possible that he now thought Burt had the better part. Actually, Burt only wanted what was best for the picture with no other agenda.

Hill and I got to work trying to find a solution. We devised a situation which we hoped Gable would accept. The meeting was held at his agent's office. We phrased our solution to Gable in such a way that it would allow him to elaborate on it and make the idea his own.

"What if you were wounded? A concussion from a depth charge making you unable to resume command?" He bought it. In fact, he offered a couple lines of dialogue.

"I get dizzy. I start to buckle. They carry me to my quarters."

"Yes, Clark. Exactly."

"And I can still hear what's going on and issue orders if necessary."

"Right, Clark. No mutiny."

Shooting resumed the next day.

The comedian, Don Rickles, was in the crew and amused the cast daily with his standard insults. No one was spared. Not Burt, not Gable, and not Harold Hecht who took it too seriously and would visit the set less often when Rickles was in a scene.

I invited my father in law, Ozzie, to come with me one day during an exciting battle scene. As he and I watched, gallons of water shot from a sound stage canon, landing on the deck where Burt and Gable were standing. Thoroughly drenched, Burt called out, "Stop! Hold it!" He stepped over to the tower railing and looked directly down at Ozzie.

Startled, Ozzie wondered, "What have I done?"

"Your son-in-law!" said Burt, soaked from head to foot and pointing now at me standing next to Ozzie, "Your son-of-a-bitch son-in-law put us up here on this godforsaken deck!" And then he grinned. Ozzie relaxed.

During filming, our son, Lawrence John, was born. In fact, Larry was almost born in our car just as we made it at five a.m. from our leased home on Mandeville Canyon to Cedars-Sinai Hospital. Gable sent a large silver piggy bank which would have made a memorable souvenir for Larry had it not been stolen later that year.

At the conclusion of principal photography, Jim Hill and I sat down to watch a rough cut. I was nervous, excited, on edge. I soon became dismayed. It seemed so...so mechanical, so inert. Many of the special effects hadn't been inserted yet, and there was no musical score. Hill was very satisfied, however, and I thought, perhaps I was being too critical. One month later, I saw the finished product and what a difference. It was my baptism into the impact a score, dubbing, looping, and special effects can have. Perhaps my first picture would have a chance.

Navy brass saw it first at a screening in Washington D.C. with a very favorable reaction. The countrywide opening on the hyped-up publicity ad led off with, "THE BIG TWO FIRE THE BIG ONE!" Reviews came two weeks later on March 28, 1958.

Bosley Crowther in *The New York Times,* "A better film about the war beneath the ocean and about the guys in the 'silent service' has not been made. It has the hard cold ring of truth." Most other reviews across the country were highly favorable, but the *New York Tribune* thought it just another Navy service picture. What mattered to H.H.L., however, was the box office. It had record breaking openings that held up very well. So well that Bobbie and I celebrated for a week. A toast to the writer. The writer? Me? Maybe. For now.

Only two years later, Gable died of a heart attack after filming *The Misfits* with Marilyn Monroe. I'll never forget his generosity in welcoming me, the new writer in town. *Run Silent, Run Deep* has been shown on television more than any other film of mine for two reasons. It's a timeless story of men in battle and no residual money had to be paid to writers and actors for television showings if a film was made before 1960.

CHAPTER 19

Unfortunately for my New York agent, Blanche Gaines, the television business was moving west to California. A dear lady in a remarkable time for new television writers, but along came the sixties. The roof caved in on her and she lost her stable. Blanche never left the business. It left her. The breakup was very traumatic for all of us. So much so in Rod Serling's case that he wrote a *Playhouse 90* about it called *The Velvet Alley* in which Blanche was played by Jack Klugman. The night of the telecast (a three hour delay in L.A.), Blanche called me from New York during a commercial to see if I was watching it.

"Bobbie and I have it on right now."

"Well. Not to spoil it for you, but I die at the end."

My representation in Hollywood became H.N. Swanson, a celebrated literary agent who at one time represented F. Scott Fitzgerald and William Faulkner. "Swannie", always in a pin stripe suit and wearing a carnation in his lapel (grown in his own garden), made the studio rounds daily representing his stable of screenwriters and selling books for adaptation to film. He had only two agents working for him in a two-story building he owned on Sunset Boulevard, a small operation compared to the other agencies of the time. And, I was soon to discover, Swannie always answered your calls.

A persuasive, colorful character, Swannie had short aphorisms for every occasion. If you took too long getting hired by a producer, "Stop dancing around the ballroom and get into bed!" His advice? "You'll get along fine in this town as long as you keep it in your pants." His major regret was his failure to sell what many called John O'Hara's greatest novel, *Appointment in Samara*. O'Hara always demanded too much money for it. It remains unsold to this day.

I had never collaborated with anyone before, but H.H.L. wanted me to work with Ray Bradbury, the celebrated novelist, playwright, and short story writer. Our assignment was to adapt a novel for the screen called *White Hunter, Black Heart* by Peter Viertel. It told of a character very much like the acclaimed director, John Huston, filming in Africa. Bradbury had never collaborated with anyone either and we soon discovered that his writing methods and mine were so different that it just wasn't going to work. I'm happy to say, we remain good friends to this day. As for *White Hunter, Black Heart*, it was finally made many years later starring Clint Eastwood and, unusual for Eastwood, was not successful.

A new distinguished drama anthology, *Playhouse 90,* was inaugurated at CBS Studios. During a short break from HHL, Playhouse 90 wanted me to lengthen my play, *The Day Before Atlanta*, to a ninety minute format. I created an additional battle scene which required a much larger studio space, and the director this time, Ralph Nelson, decided to tape the scene on location instead and then incorporate it into the live broadcast. It was, in fact, the beginning of the end for live, dramatic television plays. Tape would eventually take over the entire production.

Something happened at this point that helped to advance my writing career more than I could have ever imagined. Terrence Rattigan, the renowned British playwright, had written *Separate Tables* which was a hit on both New York and London stages. H.H.L. bought the play and Rattigan wrote a first draft, but the company thought it needed more work. I was never told why, but Rattigan declined to do a rewrite and I was given the assignment. Rattigan did come to Los Angeles, however, before filming began.

Harold invited him to go sailing on his yacht along with me, Jim Hill, and Hill's girlfriend at the time, Rita Hayworth. We were driven to the dock in San Pedro by Harold, himself, in his custom Cadillac station wagon. I had been aboard the yacht before when I worked on *Run Silent Run Deep* with Robert Wise and agreed with Harold that it was a beauty but I thought, perhaps, that Harold went too far in telling Rattigan it was the most beautiful in California.

When we arrived on the dock, there before us was a yacht gleaming in the morning sun. Only one problem. It wasn't Harold's yacht. It was larger, much larger. Rattigan stepped out of the car and exclaimed, "Harold, it's magnificent!" Jim Hill and I exchanged a glance. A few yards down the dock, we could both see Harold's yacht looking far less impressive by comparison. With some amusement, we watched Harold as he was forced to point out that the yacht before us wasn't his. Ever the gentlemen, however, Rattigan, took it in stride. "Yes, Harold. Magnificent."

Separate Tables is really two one-act plays about a group of boarders living in an English seaside resort hotel. Rattigan's play was designed so that two actors could play all four leading parts in succession on stage. With film, however, the two plays could be combined as one with special effects photography allowing two actors to play all four parts in the same time frame. That's where the trouble began.

H.H.L. wanted Laurence Olivier for the retired British Colonel, but Olivier insisted on playing the other male lead, too, a novelist, as it was done on stage. Olivier also wanted his wife, Vivian Leigh, to play both of the two female leads. I thought the idea terrific. But Burt now wanted to play the novelist which would mean eliminating the concept of two actors for four parts. With that decision, both the Oliviers left the project. David Niven was then chosen to play the British Colonel and Deborah Kerr and Rita Hayworth, the feminine leads.

A two-week rehearsal schedule was set with Delbert Mann (Del), the Academy Award winning director of *Marty.* Niven felt himself inadequate to follow Laurence Olivier, but each day of rehearsal brought him more confidence. Burt, as an alcoholic author, and Rita, as his ex-wife, played their parts quite well although unsuited to the very English atmosphere of a British seaside hotel.

Two accomplished English actresses, Gladys Cooper and Cathleen Nesbett, showed their displeasure at having a writer other than Rattigan present during rehearsals. I tried my best to overcome their animosity without success. Another British actress, Wendy Hiller, kept a copy of the original play at her side to be certain lines she liked were not eliminated, a situation somewhat analogous to Rex Harrison who kept a copy of Shaw's *Pygmalion* while rehearsing *My Fair Lady*. I was fascinated watching it slowly come together.

The entire seaside hotel was constructed on a sound stage on the Goldwyn lot. It gave the actors a reassuring feeling of being at the actual hotel. I had wanted to "open up" the story by taking it to exterior locations, but Del thought the claustrophobic atmosphere of the hotel interior was an essential part of the story. He was right. To set the mood, Harold had me write a brief prologue.

>"A seaside town on the south coast of
>England. A summer resort for the
>tourist, a winter refuge for the
>lonely, the resigned, the desperate.
>It is winter now at the Beauregard Hotel."

Separate Tables opened in December of 1958 to glowing reviews. Some compared it favorably to the stage production. The New York *Herald Tribune* critic called it one of the year's finest achievements and *The New York Times* critic, "The pathos and shabbiness of self-centered existences are harrowingly exposed."

Niven took both the Academy Award and the New York Film Critics award for Best Actor. Wendy Hiller received the Academy Best Supporting Actress award. What would be the fate of the screenplay? Bobbie and I sat in the eighth row of the Pantages theater, right on the aisle in case the film took the Oscar. Rattigan wasn't present and I really hadn't the faintest idea of what I would say.

The musical, *Gigi*, won the Oscar. Did I care? Here was my second picture, shared by fortunate circumstance with a leading playwright, and it had garnered a nomination. I was still the same writer who was about to move to a cow pasture only two years ago. Where would I go from here? As it turned out, London. For a Western.

CHAPTER 20

One of my favorite novels, *The Way West,* by A. B. Guthrie, had been purchased by H.H.L. Clifford Odets had been hired to write a script which turned out to be a three hundred page screenplay, an impossible length for a motion picture. Since H.H.L. was in London at the time filming *The Devil's Disciple* by George Bernard Shaw, I was sent there along with another screenwriter, Marvin Borowsky, to edit and completely revise the Odets' screenplay.

The Devil's Disciple had an all star cast of Burt Lancaster, Kirk Douglas, and Laurence Oliver, with Sandy MacKendrick directing. Marvin and I set to work immediately in London on Odets' script.

Invited to Harold's flat the first week to discuss changes, the doorman told us we would have to wait downstairs. "Mr. Hecht is entertaining a lady." We waited. And waited. The doorman then made an observation. "The trouble with you Americans is that you are so indiscreet about your indiscretions."

After six weeks of work, Harold and Jim Hill kept fighting with each other over the direction the script should take. We couldn't get them to agree on anything. The animosity between them reached an impasse. Harold decided to temporarily shelve the project. As for *The Devil's Disciple,* it couldn't lose. But it did. MacKendrick and Harold had artistic disagreements from the beginning. Guy Hamilton was brought on to replace Mackendrick and the result was both an artistic and commercial flop. Somehow, the words of George Bernard Shaw and this trio of superstars just didn't mix.

Back home, between assignments, I had the opportunity to write another *Playhouse 90*, live, rehearsed. This time, an original. I had always been intrigued by a line from Voltaire, "All murderers are punished unless they kill in large numbers and to the sound of trumpets." It was an ironic expression against the false glory of war and I used *To the Sound of Trumpets* as my title for a World War I drama. A strong supporting cast was assembled with Judith Anderson, Boris Karloff, and Sam Jaffe. As one of the critics later noted, "Where acting is concerned, they wrote the book." The two young leads, Stephen Boyd and Dolores Hart, created in one critic's opinion, "Incandescent love scenes". Only two or three years later, Dolores Hart left Hollywood and became a Mother Superior in Boston. I trust my play had nothing to do with it.

The reviews for *To the Sound of Trumpets* illustrate what I was up against as a screenwriter. Jack Gould of *The New York Times* wrote, "An obvious and flat drama." John Crosby of the New York *Herald Tribune* differed. "It is far and away the best *Playhouse 90* I have seen this year or, for that matter, for a good long time." What's a writer to believe? If you don't believe the bad ones, why believe the good ones? I often found myself believing neither one.

Filled with a small measure of economic confidence now, I purchased a home in Pacific Palisades just down the block from the Serlings. Carol was helping us move in when H.H.L., recovering from the failure of *The Devil's Disciple,* wanted me in Mexico for rewrites on a picture they were filming there with Lancaster and Audrey Hepburn, directed by John Huston. It took three fights and several stormy, hair-raising moments over Torreon before I finally arrived in the town of Durango.

CHAPTER 21

The Unforgiven, from a novel by Alan Le May and a filmplay by Ben Maddow, is a love story set against a background of racial bigotry about a Kiowa Indian girl, Hepburn, raised as a member of a white family with her origin kept hidden by the family's mother.

When I arrived in Durango, Jim Hill told me immediately that Huston needed a new scene to be filmed the very next morning. He wanted a big, long, gutsy speech for Charles Bickford, a homesteading neighbor of the Zacharys, whose character denied rumors that the Zachary daughter was Indian. Setting to work at once, I brought the speech to Huston that night at his rented Mexican villa, well aware that I was facing one of the notable Hollywood directors with a reputation for scathing criticism. When Jim and I arrived, we were told he was in the bathtub. We waited nervously for God knows how long and then God finally appeared in a sort of a modified safari outfit. He looked rather grim as we sat together and Jim looked on.

"You're John Gay? You wrote this?"

"I did. Yes."

He stared at me with piercing Hustonian eyes, a cigarette dangling from his mouth. I waited. "It's swell, kid. Swell." I not only felt relief, but I could see it on Jim's face, too, as it was Jim who had brought me here with his personal recommendation.

Huston went on to say that I captured the same feeling in the speech as that of the character, Ephriam, in O'Neill's *Desire Under the Elms*. I confessed that I had played the part of Ephriam in summer stock and, with that, Huston's eyes bore into me once again.

He said, "<u>You</u> played Ephriam?" in such a way that I doubted he believed me. I felt a test coming on. To my amazement, he spoke a line of Ephriam's from the play. "When ah come heah fifty odd years ago, this place waren't nothin' but fields of stone!"

He waited for me to follow up with the next line. I threw myself into the part instantly with Ephriam's New England accent.

"Folks laughed when I took it! They couldn't know what I knowed. When you can make corn sprout outta stone..."

Huston joined in. "God's living in you!"

Jim looked on with astonishment. I couldn't have made a better introductory impression. My experience as an actor didn't hurt, but how did John Huston know lines from *Desire Under the Elms?* He confided that he had never forgotten watching his father, Walter Huston, play the part on stage.

Driving to the location the next day, Huston had a Spanish-English dictionary in hand, going over some basic Spanish words. This puzzled me as he had already directed one of the finest Westerns ever made, *Treasure of Sierra Madre,* shot in Mexico. In addition, I heard that he had once fought with the Mexican cavalry against the banditos in the Mexican hills. Was it all bullshit? He certainly was a very complex man and I couldn't wait to see him at work.

The speech I wrote for Bickford required two actors to play in the scene with him. As there was no one on the location to play them, Huston cast me on the spot along with Jim Hill. Acting? I was going to be acting again? Giving us no direction at all, Huston shot the scene. He then said, "Swell. Print it." One take. I couldn't believe it.

Bickford came up to me afterwards, beaming, and congratulated me. Was it for my acting? I thanked him but, alas, it was for the speech I'd written for him, not my performance.

I was soon to learn that Huston filmed a lot of single takes. There also seemed to be little communication between him and the cast. Just a lot of "Swells". If an actor didn't feel comfortable and asked for direction, Huston's answer would be, "Do it again." Huston, one of the great film directors. I couldn't get over how little discussion was given to actors in terms of their characters. I heard later that he wanted his actors to be unencumbered by thoughts of the director. It was certainly different from the custom of theater directors who discuss character relationships in a play before the actors appear in front of an audience.

I felt that Audrey Hepburn, playing a teenaged Kiowa girl, was unusual casting for the part. A <u>Kiowa</u>? Huston looked for ways to make her more physically acceptable. In a scene where she looks at herself in the mirror, I told Huston it might be a good idea to have her take the soot from a nearby lamp on the bureau and rub it across her forehead.

"Exactly. That's it. Swell." Then Huston turned a contemptuous eye on the art director next to me with a caustic, "Why the hell didn't <u>you</u> think of that?" That was Huston. Praising one person and humiliating another at the same time.

He had a way of using the camera unlike anything I had seen before. Instead of the standard long shots and close shots and over the shoulder shots, he would combine them all in one continuous shot, letting the actors move to planned positions rather than the camera. Later, I discovered his motive for this unique method of filming. It prevented studio heads from editing his work. They were limited to far fewer shots from which to choose. In effect, it offered Huston a final cut.

Local Mexicans in the area were hired to portray Kiowas threatening the family in their soddy. At lunch time, every one ate in a huge tent constructed on location, except the local Mexicans. They were not allowed to join the company of actors and technicians and were told to bring their own food. They could then pick up any company food left over. Finally, Hill ordered the production manager to have them eat with the rest of us. The production manager was reluctant, noting that it would set a precedent for the next film crew using Durango for a location. Hill, to his credit, replied, "That's just what I want to do."

One incident I'll never forget. An old Mexican Indian, who must have been in his eighties with a marvelous face of bronze, was asked to play the Kiowa war chief on the next day's shooting. He was instructed to ride up to the soddy and raise his arm in defiance. A stunt man would then take over in the same chief's costume and, upon being shot, fall to his death from the horse. When the old man arrived the next day, we discovered that he told his family he would not be returning home. He said the movie people were paying him to be shot from a horse and killed. The money for it was more than he had ever earned in his entire life. He was ready to make the sacrifice. Huston, Burt, Jim, and I could hardly believe it, but he was absolutely serious. I still remember the old man's face, overwhelmed with relief, when John told him he didn't have to die, that the money would still be his.

Joseph Wiseman, a gaunt, lanky, and very resourceful character actor from the New York theater, played the villain, an "Injun hater". Joe had never come near a horse in New York, but being an actor who researches every part, he was determined to learn. One day, driving to the set, Jim and I saw a distant figure riding across the desert. We took off in his direction across the brush and there was Joe Wiseman, plodding along on a horse that looked as dismal and weary as Joe.

"Move on," said Joe, barely glancing at us. "Move on. Just another wandering Jew."

Lillian Gish, a great star of the silent films, played the mother. She had expressive eyes and used them to striking effect in the days when film had no sound. Now, however, they seemed too expressive. In one scene, the camera was on her reaction in close-up to a lynching when the film ran out. Huston gestured to the cameraman. "Never mind. Just let her keep going. Those eyes."

Burt leaned close to me and suggested that I add a line to the scene when the family's under attack from the Kiowas. "Close your eyes, Mama, you're

Chapter Twenty-One

giving away our position!" He wasn't serious, of course. Dear Lillian.

There was a line in Lillian's part that remained from the book. A confession in which she reveals having lost her own child at birth, she took the Indian baby as her own. It was a very overwrought line and I feared Gish might overdo it. "Mah breasts were hurtin' with all that milk." Huston insisted on keeping the line and, for once, had her saying it for several takes until he was satisfied. Audie Murphy's comment afterward, "I never claimed to be an actor but if that's acting, then I'm Laurence Olivier."

Huston decided that the last love scene between Burt and Audrey just wasn't working. It had to be filmed that afternoon. I set to work with my portable Royal on an overturned orange crate and rewrote the scene. Huston still didn't like it. Neither did Burt. I sat down again with my portable and wrote a second version. Huston? Didn't like it. And neither did Burt. Once again, back to my Royal. This time, Huston gave me his favorite one word approval. "Swell". Burt just shook his head as he turned on me. "Why the hell didn't you write this the <u>first</u> time?"

The Unforgiven opened to fair reviews. I didn't receive a film credit and didn't expect one. Many times, even more so today, studio execs hire several writers for a single picture. The result often brings about arbitrations over whose name or names should be on the screen. It's a difficult, painful process for all concerned with thousands of bonus dollars at stake. The decision is made by experienced qualified members of the Writers Guild after reading all of the material involved. Studio execs, I'm happy to say, are not permitted to have a part in the decision.

As for *The Unforgiven*, the critics declared it not to be Huston's better work. A few found it an unusually sensitive Western about racism. The premise of an Indian woman being abducted by whites rather than the reverse. In looking back, I felt that Huston was never comfortable in the course of making the picture. A strange man in so many ways. Mr. Charm with a brutal streak.

CHAPTER 22

One last *Playhouse 90* project came to me from Herb Brodkin, a television adaptation of *Out Of Dust* from a play by Lynn Riggs. Riggs was the author of *Green Grow the Lilacs,* from which the musical *Oklahoma* was adapted. The lead was played by Uta Hagen, one of the revered actresses of the American theater. In rehearsal, I immediately found out why.

In order to understand her character better, she asked me to write a three page biography of the character up to the moment the play began. That night, I stayed up late and wrote four pages of what I imagined the character had been through in the past. The next morning, I gave her the pages and watched her read through them. I couldn't gauge any kind of reaction, but then she approached and hugged me. It was better than any words she might say. If only all actresses could be that dedicated. The reviews for *Out Of Dust* claimed it further enhanced the reputation of *Playhouse 90*.

H.H.L. was doing so well at the time that they were offered a contract, I was told, to take over MGM if Burt would agree to star in *Ben Hur*. He refused. Or, more to the point, H.H.L. refused, unwilling to dismantle a very successful independent company. Now, however, dissension among them was beginning to grow with a lot of heated arguments. I can remember going down the hall one day and seeing Burt literally lift the diminutive Harold right off the floor by the front of his jacket. It startled me. Right off the floor!

Harold called me over to his house one night to discuss a possible project and I happened to arrive in the midst of a screening, *Bus Stop*. I thought it best to remain silent until the picture was over. A mistake.

When the lights came up, Gloria rose with fire in her eyes and marched directly over to me.

"You sonofabitch! You can't even say hello when you come in? Who the hell do you think you are!" Echoes of Gloria's angry voice came back to me from that time on the yacht off Catalina. I mumbled something and she left the room. It was obvious that she and Harold must have had a major quarrel earlier in the evening.

Harold sighed and said to me, "Let's take a walk. A little night air might help."

We strolled around the block and when we returned to the house, Gloria had locked all the doors. Harold didn't have a key and couldn't get in. It didn't seem to disturb him very much. It had happened before. He said he'd walk over to the Beverly Hills Hotel, only three blocks away, and stay there for the night.

At H.H.L., the dissension grew worse and was clearly leading to a breakup. When it came, it was like a bitter divorce with everyone deciding who should get what literary properties that the company owned. I even heard, though it was never confirmed, that Harold's yacht really didn't belong to him. That without Burt's knowledge, it belonged to the company.

Harold left the building on Canon Drive and rented an office in Beverly Hills. My HHL days were over, but Harold came up with a strange request. Did I know any dog stories? The only one I could think of was *Greyfriars Bobby*, a book about a small Skye terrier who refused to leave his master's grave.

Harold was immediately interested. "Give me the pitch."

It was fairly simple. When the dog's master died, the Skye terrier stood watch over his grave for fourteen years, touching the hearts of the townspeople. Eventually, they built a shelter for him next to the grave and he left it only for food. The little dog became a legend and when he died, a bronze statue was created which still stands today at Greyfriars graveyard in Edinburgh, Scotland.

Harold responded, "Empathy! Heart!"

"But why?" I asked, "Do you want a dog story?" His response floored me. Even for Harold.

"I can get the hottest dog in town right now for a fantastic price. Everybody loves this dog!"

"What dog?" I asked.

"The Shaggy Dog. A star dog." It had been in a successful film called The *Absent Minded Professor* and the dog wasn't working at the moment. I confessed to Harold that I had never seen the picture, but I understood it was a huge sheep dog while Greyfriars Bobby was a small Skye terrier. Harold wasn't persuaded. He'd run the picture for me that night while he was reading the Greyfriars book. "See you tomorrow."

It was Harold Hecht who brought me out here. Gave me my start. I owed him that much. That night, I watched the film in a sort of incomprehensible daze. The Shaggy Dog was not only huge, it could talk.

The next morning, Harold told me that he loved the book. I was beginning to feel like a character in one of Rod's Twilight Zones when I said firmly, "Harold, this dog talks and he's not small."

"So what? He can speak to his master at the grave. We'll get a voice-over." This was getting very bizarre.

"It isn't a comedy, Harold. It's profoundly touching. Nothing cute. Nothing funny."

"So what? An audience will expect him to talk."

"No. Not Greyfriars Bobby!"

For the next five minutes we argued over star dogs, comedy, drama, audiences, and I felt that I was losing it. He was quite serious and wanted me to work up an outline for a screenplay. I told him that I'd certainly give it some thought. As it turned out, I gave it so much thought that the project was dropped.

CHAPTER 23

I now had a house with a huge mortgage, two small children, one on the way, and the collapse of H.H.L. It was getting a little scary with a Writers Guild strike beginning when a call came in to adapt a book Jim Hill had optioned. Jim had signed a favored nation agreement to adhere to any settlement from the strike and wanted me to start immediately. *The Oldest Confession,* by Richard Condon, is a story of three crooks who dare to steal a Goya painting from the Prado museum in Madrid, written with unique style. It was a delightful assignment and my first draft came quickly. Jim started casting within weeks of submitting it. He signed Rex Harrison for the lead, co-starring Rita Hayworth who was now Jim's wife. With filming about to begin in Madrid under George Marshall's direction, Jim called me in Los Angeles to say some last minute rewrites were necessary.

Three days later, I arrived in Madrid and was told that Harrison insisted I be at the airport the following day to meet him when he arrived. Jim arranged to have a car pick me up at the hotel and take me to the airport. I was ready that morning, but the car never appeared. I ran into Jim in the hotel lobby. "Where were you?" he exploded. "Rex is pissed off you weren't at the airport. It's no way to start off with him."

The last thing I wanted to do at this point was to piss off Rex Harrison. There was no one I admired more. Hill relayed my apologies, explaining the limousine company was at fault.

We met that evening in the hotel cocktail lounge where I repeated my apology. Harrison seemed cordial and made no mention of my absence at the airport. My big concern at the moment was his reaction to the script. He said he liked it. Not effusive, but he liked it.

"I have one problem," he said. "My character's name. It's written James or Jamey in the script. Now I'm told the Spanish call me Hy-mie."

"That's right," I explained, "Jamey is, indeed, pronounced Hy-mie by the Spanish." Harrison looked at me with that quizzical tilt of the head I'd seen before on stage and screen.

"Hy-mie? Hy-mie? Are you certain?"

I tried to assure him that it was the Spanish pronunciation of the name. He looked to Jim for confirmation. Jim nodded.

"Really," said Rex. "Hy-mie. It sounds Jewish. Do you think we ought to do that?"

I told him that the Spanish pronunciation would really have to be used. "The story does take place in Spain."

"Hymie?" He seemed disturbed, but we kept it.

On the way back to my room, I happened to see Tyrone Power in the hotel elevator, looking as he did on film, impossibly handsome. A prominent star for twenty years, he was working in Spain on a film, *Solomon and Sheba*. The following morning, I was shocked to hear that Power had suffered a heart attack and died. He'd only been filming for a week and, by the following week, they replaced him with Yule Brynner. Too much money at stake. It seemed abrupt, to say the least.

Just before leaving Madrid, I was still working on rewrites at the airport with Jim Hill and George Marshall. In fact, they had the Spanish authorities hold my flight for an hour, allowing me to complete them in the airport lounge. The power of celebrity and a movie company. I'll never forget the dagger looks from the passengers as I walked down the aisle of the aircraft.

The title of *The Oldest Confession* was changed by the studio to *The Happy Thieves* and filmed in black and white. In hindsight, I felt there were two mistakes made at the inception. The first was signing George Marshall to direct. Noted for his broad slapstick comedies, he was an unfortunate choice to direct Harrison, one of the wittiest, sophisticated actors in the British theater.

The second mistake was the casting of Rita Hayworth. I recall how difficult it was communicating with her. So guarded now, withdrawn. Jim knew she was an alcoholic and others suspected. But no one knew then she was starting the very first step on the long slow road of Alzheimer's disease. She was not the vivacious Rita we knew from her films and it affected her performance. A few generous critics called the picture "lighthearted" but "tepid" was the more general comment. To me, it was a huge disappointment. I felt personally that I had let down the author of the book, Richard Condon. So many elements enter into adaptations, the screenplay in particular, and I rightly blamed myself as well as others.

CHAPTER 24

Before *The Happy Thieves* was released, the 1960 strike was over. Out of it, for the first time, pension, health, and welfare benefits were instituted which still continue with improvements every year. MGM offered me a multiple picture contract at a time when such deals were being phased out. My good fortune was due to Bernie Smith, my former script editor at Hecht-Hill-Lancaster, who was now an MGM producer. I still had fond memories of my discussions with Bernie which included the unfortunate circumstance of his initialed shirts. When he made a strong point with conviction, I couldn't help avoiding the "B.S." so plainly visible on his breast pocket.

I was no sooner settled in an office when they had me look at a film in progress. Not just any film, but one presently shooting in a new process called Cinerama. It employed three cameras filming simultaneously and later projected together on a giant wide screen. The effect was astonishing, but it had two fatal flaws. The projection couldn't completely eliminate lines where the three film strips came together, and very few theaters had the equipment to exhibit it.

How the West Was Won was the tentative title from a script by Jim Webb who conceived the idea from a *Life* magazine article, "The Winning of the West". His script had six time segments, three of which had already been filmed and remained as shot. Huge rewrites were required on the remaining ones. Three directors were hired for the picture but Henry Hathway, the notable veteran director, was responsible for the major part of the work.

MGM scheduled a screening for me to see the footage up to date. I made notes, met with Henry Hathaway, and began the rewrites which had to be finished on an accelerated schedule.

Already appearing in the first segment were James Stewart, Henry Fonda, Debbie Reynolds, John Wayne, and Karl Malden. Filming would soon begin on the second segment with Gregory Peck, Robert Preston, and Debbie Reynolds. It was my understanding that all actors' contracts called for them to receive equal pay under a special arrangement which included a contribution to a charity. The total price without this proviso would have been staggering.

I was told that John Wayne, who had a brief appearance in the third sequence directed by John Ford, wanted an additional payment now for the last sequence which wasn't called for in his contract. He didn't get it and walked off the picture. Henry then had me rewrite his part for the actor, Lee J. Cobb. A very young George Peppard played the juvenile lead in the sequence with Cobb. Peppard blamed MGM for Wayne walking out. Peppard was wrong, but then I found him a very dislikable fellow in any case. A star attitude beyond the capability of his talent.

Observing Hathaway on location in Arizona, I saw the three Cinerama cameras in action. They had to be within inches of the actors in order to film close-ups. Henry was forever chewing on his cigar and chewing out anyone, star or grip, if he felt they weren't performing their best. Together, we worked out a runaway train sequence, almost frame by frame, for the last part of the picture which is still regarded today as a landmark action sequence. It's true that Henry deserved the reputation of being an irascible director, but he was also a masterful cinematic one and I developed a great affection for him.

MGM gave the picture a huge promotion with a star studded premiere in Hollywood. The reviews were mixed, but the crowds loved it and today, the box office would mark it as a blockbuster. I put in for a shared writing credit with Jim Webb who felt that he deserved a single credit. The usual procedure is to write a letter to the Guild arbitrators explaining your position for a credit and then abide by their decision. In this case, Jim convinced me to write a joint letter from both of us with our positions. I lost the arbitration. Jim did, however, thank me publicly on Oscar night when *How the West Was Won* received the Academy Award for best screenplay. Hathaway went around telling everyone I was robbed. I made no such statements. Why complain? MGM was more than satisfied with my work.

The Writers Guild called to ask me if I would join the Board of Directors temporarily until Eric Ambler, the well-known writer of suspense novels, returned from London. I was floored by the offer. It was an honor to accept the position. Ambler wired the Board stating it was his understanding that if he didn't return for the next meeting, his name would be John Gay. He returned. My work for the Guild still lay ahead.

CHAPTER 25

With the first film under my belt, it wasn't long before Bernie told me that MGM had another rewrite for me, a picture ready to shoot in Paris with Glenn Ford.

"Get on a plane, you leave tomorrow."

"What if I don't like the script?"

"Hey, it's only two short love scenes. That's all they want."

"I know, but what if I don't...?"

"The director is Vincente Minnelli."

"I'll go."

The film was an updated version of the World War I silent film, *The Four Horsemen of the Apocalypse,* with a script that had been changed to World War II.

Bobbie was not at all thrilled with my leaving as our third child was due in two weeks. I promised I'd be back in time. Only two scenes.

Air France had a cocktail lounge on the plane at that time with a mahogany bar, eight bar stools, a uniformed bartender, fish tank, and several leather lounge chairs. It was a smooth flight and I soon sat back to read the script for the first time. To my dismay, it turned out there were several love scenes in the script, and I didn't like any of them. Which two did they have in mind? Worse than that, I wasn't very keen on the entire script. What the hell would I say when I arrived? Be circumspect? Diplomatic? I decided I'd ask them which two scenes they wanted rewritten and do my best. By no means would I tell them what I really thought of the entire script. After all, they were ready to shoot in two weeks. And this was Vincente Minnelli!

Jet lagged, I checked into the Georges V Hotel and went immediately to the Minnelli suite. In spite of my exhaustion, I was excited to meet Minnelli and the producer, Julian Blaustein. Minnelli, gracious as we met but also tenacious, didn't waste much time before he posed the first question.

"How did you like the script?"

I avoided the question by immediately asking which scenes they wanted rewritten. But Minnelli was insistent.

"How did you like the script?"

I admitted that I did have a little problem with it.

But I'd be happy to work on the two love scenes. "Which two?"

Minnelli leaned forward as he faced me. "You didn't like the script." A pause. "Why?"

The dreaded moment had arrived. I was certainly not sent here to rock the boat. A six million dollar production set to go. Today it would be over a hundred million. Again, I tried to find out which two love scenes they wanted rewritten. Minnelli would have none of it.

I tried another tactic. "Perhaps I could rewrite whatever love scenes that trouble you."

Minnelli remained persistent, "And the <u>rest</u> of the script?"

I had to confess that I did think it needed some additional work.

Minnelli leaned forward once again. "You don't like it. You don't like any of it." And then he turned to Blaustein. "You see? I told you it needed work. A <u>lot</u> of work!"

At this moment, all I wanted to do was bow out. Wish them luck and go. Minnelli had other ideas. He insisted that I start immediately on page one.

"Rewrite everything you feel needs work."

Blaustein looked grim. In fact, he appeared just as miserable as I felt. His director was asking for a complete rewrite? I told Blaustein that it really might be better if they brought in another writer who might have a more positive outlook on the script. With this, Minnelli became more adamant than ever.

"No. Go to work. Start now."

Blaustein was about to fly to Sweden the next day and sign Ingrid Thulin for the feminine lead. He was worried about the changes Minnelli and I might work out in his absence. Minnelli assured him that every change would be open to his review. I still wanted to get on a plane as soon as possible and get the hell back home. Not a chance. Not anymore. At the end of the meeting, I was calling Minnelli Vincente and Blaustein Julie. It was Julie who came up with one very wise suggestion which I wish I had taken that day. Avoid the onion soup at lunch. It came up, too.

With Julie gone, jet lagged, I worked hours into the night on the first scene. I had never wished for a negative reaction to my work, especially from someone like Vincente Minnelli, but I did now. As it turned out, he loved the rewrites and was even more determined to keep me on.

I had completed a week of rewrites when Bobbie called from California to say the baby would be arriving early. "Come home!"

Vincente said, "One week. And I want you back!"

Elizabeth Ann arrived on Sunday afternoon. Another girl! She interrupted the attending doctor's rapt attention on a televised football game. Five days later, I reluctantly returned to Paris.

Relations between Julie and Vincente had deteriorated by this time and they were hardly speaking to each other. Julie was on the top floor of the Georges V and Vincente on the ground floor. I spent a lot of time on the elevator. Up and down, back and forth, like a marriage counselor... rewriting as filming began.

Minnelli's direction is noted for his artistic composition in every shot. I found that out for myself almost immediately. In one scene, the two lovers stroll the gardens of Versailles and speak with despair of the falling autumn leaves.

As it was now spring in France, Vincente ordered dozens of autumn leaves attached to several trees. I could have easily changed the scene, but Minnelli wouldn't hear of it. When it came to visuals, he was uncompromising.

During the filming, Vincente's daughter, Liza, arrived from a boarding school in Switzerland to visit. I think she was around sixteen at the time. Effervescent and charming, you could sense her talent even then. And you could also sense they adored each other. That deep affection continued until the day he died.

All the filming that was needed on the French locations was finally completed. The remaining work would have to be done in California. Back home again, I was told to keep writing. I couldn't help thinking of my original assignment. Just two little love scenes.

Our return didn't improve the Minnelli-Blaustein relations. Sol Siegel, the MGM studio head, continued to use me as a constant mediator between them. Elaborate sets had been built on studio sound stages and on the back lot of MGM. They'd even recreated the Champs Elysees with the Arc de Triomphe in the background. After seeing the real monument in Paris, it was startling to watch it reproduced so authentically in Culver City. The monument was used to film the same historic newsreel footage of Nazi troops arriving in Paris which showed Parisians weeping along the boulevard as the Nazi troops marched along. MGM wanted to use the actual boulevard and monument to film, but was told it would be too traumatic for Parisians to relive it again.

Vincente, always into artistic composition, demanded everything be in its place. In one scene, Cobb and Glenn Ford were seated side by side in the cockpit mockup of a private airplane. Vincente was unhappy with the position of a dead deer lying prone on a shelf behind the actors. He had it moved and shot the scene again. Still not right. Moved it again and shot the scene again. Not right. By this time, the actors were getting very irate. Once again, the deer was moved and the scene filmed. And one more. Cobb finally rose up shouting, "What the hell is this fucking scene all about? The two of us or the fucking deer?" Vincente smiled. "One more. Action!"

Because of his artistic sensitivity and an effeminate manner, most people I knew thought that Vincente was gay but I never saw any evidence of it.

A serious problem remained before the release of the picture. The studio thought Ingrid Thulin's Swedish accent was difficult to understand. I didn't agree. In secrecy, unbilled, Angela Lansbury was brought in to dub her lines. Lansbury was one of our theater's best actresses, a legend by now, and too worthy to be used like this as a voice for another fine actress.

The picture opened to fair-poor reviews which reflected, for the most part, an incoherent script by Robert Ardrey and John Gay. I agreed. There was never enough time. The shooting schedule could not be delayed. Minnelli never blamed me. In fact, he rather liked the picture and did some brilliant work in many of the scenes. Blaustein, too, felt the picture deserved a better reception. But I knew that he and Vincente would never make another picture together and they didn't.

Early years...my first close-up.

Bret Harte Junior High, *The Princess Marries the Page*. My royal first stage performance in 1938.

Portraying Abie in *Abie's Irish Rose*, 1941. I'm the guy in the middle.

The Boothbay Playhouse, my shrine from 1945-1949.

Three Coast Guard gobs on weekend liberty in Central Park.

Backstage at the Boothbay Playhouse. When aging was necessary.

A summer stock staple, *Arsenic and Old Lace*. First time on stage with Bobbie, my future wife.

Gifted perhaps. Rocketing? Never.

With Harvey Marlowe, the man who sold us to
WOR from a five minute audition sketch, 1949.

Facing each other and WOR-TV and all of New York.

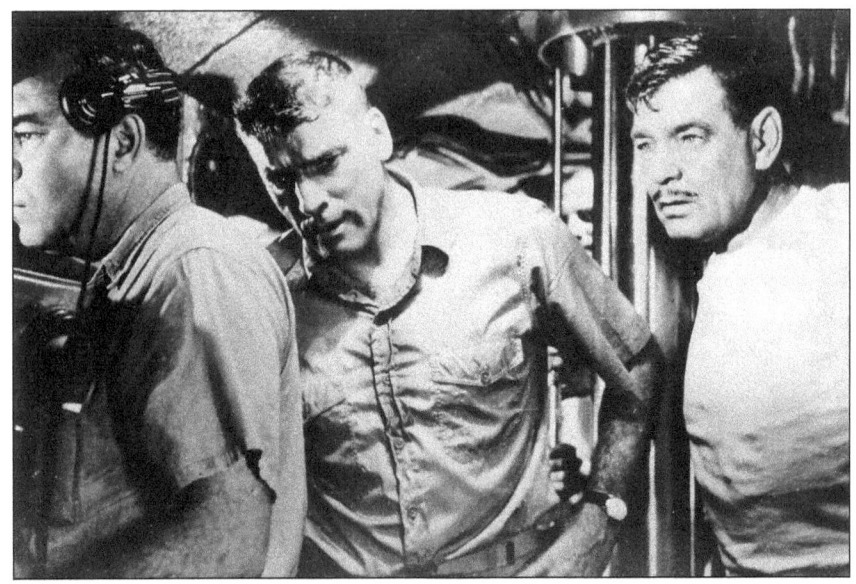

An ad for *Run Silent, Run Deep* proclaimed, "The Big Two Fire the Big One!"

With the vibrant, great director, John Sturges, discussing *The Hallelujah Trail*.

Somewhere in Tazanika for *The Last Safari* with ever-observant hunter and his pipe, 1967.

Backstage at *Diversions and Delights*, opening week on Broadway.
The smiles came from a successful tour.

Playing doctor in an Oregon hospital on *Sometimes A Great Notion*. My scene, mostly cut.

Getting my point across to a brilliant actress, Marian Mercer, who played my aunt in *Summer Voices*.

Olivia Hussey, a little apprehensive, when cornered by Norman Rosemont and me while filming *Ivanhoe*.

An overwrought ad for an Emmy-winning performance by Anthony Hopkins as Hitler in *The Bunker*.

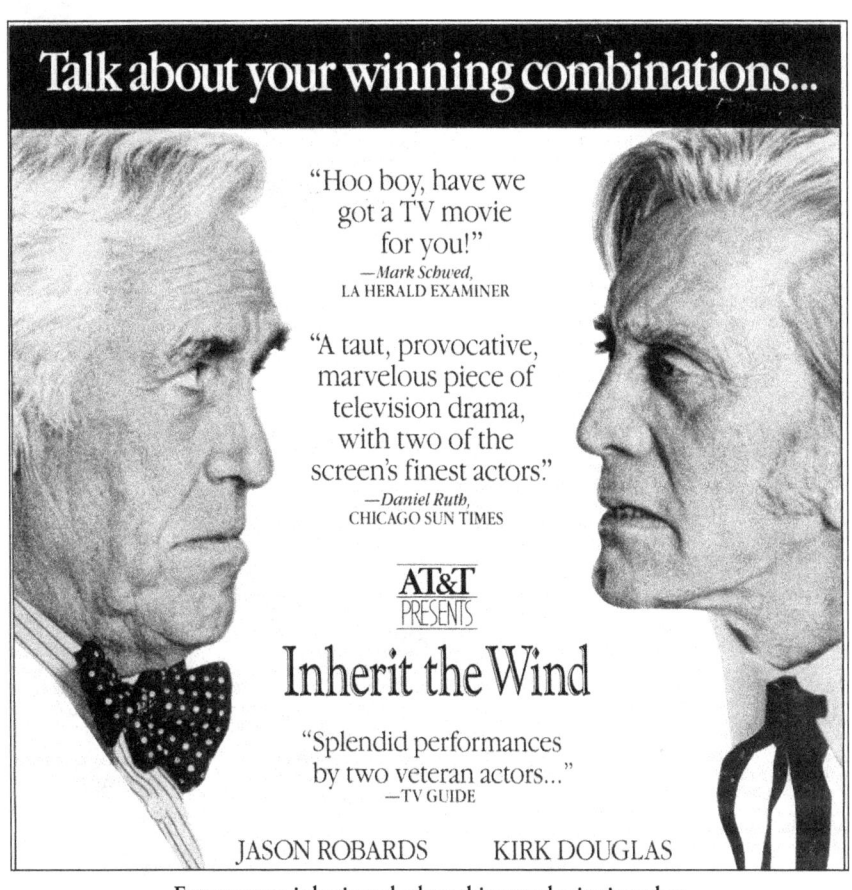

Fortunate to inherit and adapt this award-winning play.

Thrilled to team up again with the magnificent Anthony Hopkins for *The Hunchback of Notre Dame*.

CHAPTER 26

I was hoping to get an assignment from MGM in its initial stage versus another rewrite. It came, unfortunately, from a project that John Houseman was developing, and I say unfortunately because I not only disliked the novel, I had no idea of what to do with it. I certainly didn't want to get into another untenable situation after *The Four Horsemen,* so I informed the script supervisor at MGM, Milton Beecher, that I'd have to take a pass on this one. Its subject matter, that of a boring couple, was...boring. The thing is you can only turn down so many assignments under a multiple picture contract and, therefore, you don't turn them down lightly. Milton advised me to think it over carefully as Houseman was a very important producer, both in theater and film. With this warning, I read it twice, and I still didn't like it. "Get me out of it, Milton. Just tell Mr. Houseman that I'm not the right person to adapt it."

The next day, word came that Mr. Houseman still wanted to see me. This was going to be a problem. Houseman must really love the novel and I didn't want to be put in the position of saying how dull and undramatic I thought it was. Once again, I begged off the interview. Houseman remained insistent. He would like to hear my objections. I was practically forced to meet him at his office.

I started off in a low key with how much I admired him. And I did. When the subject of the book was brought up, he said, "I understand you're having some problems with the story."

"The subject matter," I replied, "is something that I don't easily identify with." To myself I said, "Bad start. I just ended a sentence with a preposition."

"Why not?" he inquired. "You just finished *The Four Horsemen,* plus a large scale Western, and you have an Academy Award nomination for *Separate Tables.* It seems to me that you identify with various subjects quite easily."

I felt myself getting in deeper. "Well, you see, Mr. Houseman, these characters in the novel I find a little... well...shallow."

"SHALLOW?" he asked. "Why?"

In a bumbling response, I got in even deeper. There was really no way out. Within a few minutes, one thing led to another and I just came right out and said it.

"It's boring. It's confusing. It's undramatic!"

I uttered all of the criticisms that I had hoped to avoid. In fact, I did everything but ask him why the hell he wanted to produce this crap!

His voice was soft. A deadly smile. "Thank you, Mr. Gay. Nice of you to come by."

It was clear that John Houseman was determined to make this picture. And he did. The picture was called *In the Cool of the Day.* It starred Peter Finch and Jane Fonda. I say with no animosity, but some self-justification, that it was a flop artistically and financially.

CHAPTER 27

Two rewrites, a turn down, and finally, finally, a project I loved. MGM had purchased a Pulitzer Prize winning novel by Robert Lewis Taylor called *The Travels of Jaimie McPheeters*. It was a most endearing story of a boy and his father who cross the broad expanses of the American West in search of fame and fortune in the California gold rush. Full of thieves, rogues, and cutthroats, it was told with wit and humor similar to the works of Mark Twain.

The norm for writers working at MGM was about three pages a day. If you wrote more than that, it was a reflection on the working habits of those who accomplished less. I felt somewhat traitorous if I turned in more than three. If MGM just dropped the hours bullshit and the pages bullshit and let us work at home, the whole process would have worked far better.

While busy on *Jamie McPheeters* one day, I had a call from Glenn Ford to meet him for lunch at the commissary. It was most unusual as Ford had always been rather cool when we were working on *The Four Horsemen of the Apocalypse*. Over a ham sandwich, I discovered his new interest in me. He wanted a note inserted in the *Jamie McPheeters* script. When describing the father, he asked if I would put in "A Glenn Ford type". The studio heads would find it a strong endorsement to cast Ford. I was thrown off balance by the request even though I thought he'd be good for the part. I began to realize that star actors have to keep actively promoting their careers.

I never included the note as the script never got to the point of casting. The budget for it came in at over seven million which MGM thought was far too much for a comedic Western about a father and son. Solution from MGM. Make it a television series. I'd simply have to edit the first thirty pages and turn them into a TV pilot. Robert Sparks was hired to produce and casting began. Glenn Ford was no longer interested as star actors did not go on television in those days. Dan O'Herlihy, an Irish actor who had appeared in my *Playhouse 90, To the Sound of Trumpets,* was cast instead. He was excellent in *Trumpets* and miscast in *McPheeters*. Kurt Russell played the son, ten at the time, just the age of the boy in the novel.

The entire TV pilot was shot on the MGM backlot when there was a backlot instead of today's houses and condos. A luncheon stroll on that back lot could take you through a Belgian hamlet, a Southern plantation, a Chinese village, endless stairways that led to nowhere, and a New York street where Gene Kelly danced in the rain.

I had written just two more episodes of *McPheeters* when MGM purchased a delightful novel called *The Courtship of Eddie's Father* and assigned Joe Pasternak, responsible for many successful MGM musicals and comedies, to produce it. Pasternak was Hungarian with an accent to match. "Give me an outline first so I can maul it over." Under contract to MGM, I was chosen to write the screenplay. I felt an outline unnecessary this time, but it was the outline that sparked the interest of Vincente Minnelli who later signed on. The story of a boy whose mother had recently died doesn't sound like a comedy. But the events that follow, as he searches for a new mother, become a spring board for honest emotion as well as amusement. This was especially true with the casting of Ron Howard, then Ronny Howard.

Glenn Ford played the father and there was no need this time for a note stating a Glenn Ford type. He was flat out right for the part. We had what might be called a "happy shoot". No outside locations, just the MGM sound stages. Shirley Jones, Dina Merrill, and Jerry Van Dyke filled out the cast. Liza Minnelli, still in her teens, helped to choreograph a scene of screaming tots at the boy's birthday party. I brought my own ten-year-old, Jennifer, to watch the filming one day. Unfortunately, she fell in love with acting. As the song goes, "Life upon the wicked stage ain't nothin' what a girl supposes."

The Courtship of Eddie's Father was previewed at a theater on Pico Boulevard not too far from the MGM studio and, if the laughter of the audience that night was any indication, Pasternak could count on another successful film. It was an audience pleaser, and it also collected some very positive reviews. In fact, I've received more royalties from subsequent TV screenings of *The Courtship of Eddie's Father* than any film I've written. It also led to a television series lasting four years, but unfortunately I had no part in it. The TV producer, James Komack, happened to be a writer.

CHAPTER 28

Working at MGM, I encountered Julie Blaustein on the lot and he challenged me to quit smoking for a day. I took the challenge. One day and then another. Two weeks later I knew I would never go back. Bobbie followed suit and 1964 became a very important year for that if nothing else.

Jim Hill and Harold Hecht came back into my life. They had a book called *The Rose of Tibet*, by Lionel Davidson, about the invasion of Tibet by the Chinese. It was a deeply moving, memorable love story in a time of historical adventure. Nothing I've done before or since can match the pleasure I had in adapting it. They sent my script to several studios, but there was a built-in obstacle to a production of it. The spectacle scenes would cost too much money. I still have hopes it might reach the screen one day. My disappointment was somewhat lessened by writing a television drama for the BBC in London. On my first night there, I secured a ticket to the play, *Alfie*, by Bill Naughton, which was produced later as a film making a star of Michael Caine.

Just a few seats down from me in the fifth row, I could see Elizabeth Taylor and Richard Burton seated together. Although Burton wasn't in the play, he was heard clearly at one point during the second act. Alfie, having just made love to one of his women, turned to the audience and said, "You know, I always feel right frisky after a romp in the hay." From the audience came Burton's sonorous voice, "Hear! Hear!" Astonishment. Silence. And then again, "Hear! Hear!" This time there was laughter as the audience realized who was speaking. The actor playing Alfie, John Neville, looked across the footlights toward the famous voice from the fifth row. Then he turned quickly about and continued with the play. He obviously didn't want any competition from Richard Burton.

Returning home, I stopped off in New York to see the Gilroys. Frank had been working on getting a play produced called *The Subject Was Roses*. The budget for the Broadway opening was fifty thousand, achieved with difficulty, yet miniscule by today's standards. We were all blissfully overwhelmed when Frank went on to receive the Pulitzer Prize and Tony Awards.

CHAPTER 29

An offer came in from a very successful independent outfit, The Mirisch Company, to write a script from a Western novel, *The Hallelujah Train*, by Bill Gullick. It would be directed by John Sturges who had just helmed the successful *The Great Escape*. The story, a satirical comedy, begins when a huge shipment of whiskey scheduled to be transported west has to be protected by troops of the United States Cavalry. Joining them on the trek is a women's temperance club, Irish teamsters, and a wily, clever tribe of Indians attracted by the whiskey shipment.

I met with John and worked out an outline with him which flowed easily as we were both in agreement on the course of the screenplay. In fact, we read many of my scenes together and he even wanted me to play one of the featured parts, a thought immediately turned down by Walter Mirisch. Burt Lancaster was signed for the Cavalry Captain and Lee Remick, the Temperance woman.

In the course of the filming, the title had been changed to *The Hallelujah Trail* for a legal reason that was never clear to me. I joined Sturges on location in Gallup, New Mexico, on the day that a stunt man was killed, falling off a covered wagon during a stampede sequence. I'm always amazed at the risks stuntmen take, but it's a way of life they've chosen and they seem to like the challenge.

Post-production work on *The Hallelujah Trail* was completed with a sparkling score by Elmer Bernstein. A screening was held privately at the Cinerama Dome Theater in Hollywood. Seeing it for the first time, I was disturbed. It seemed too long and some of the comedy scenes were played too broadly. I recalled Mark Reed's sage advice when I played in *Petticoat Fever* at the Boothbay Playhouse. Never push for laughs. Play it straight. Burt and Lee were fine...just right, but other actors were, at times, pushing. However, with further editing, I felt any problems could be alleviated, if not eliminated. My feeling about any changes, however, was not shared by the Mirisch brothers and Sturges.

The picture had a huge premiere on both coasts. Bobbie and I attended the one in Los Angeles, complete with a tent set up behind the Cinerama Theater for a Western-themed party. The audience reacted favorably, but I still felt it was too long and the comedy much too broad in places. The reviews in the trade papers, *Variety* and the *Hollywood Reporter,* were both excellent. "Funny – Exciting - Laughs and thrills". I breathed a sigh of relief until the New York reviews came in. Two or three good ones, but others were far less than enthusiastic. My own criticisms were echoed by their words.

The fact is if a writer is lucky enough to get some favorable reviews, and I do call it luck many times, more work is offered because producers feel they are taking less of a chance. If a show fails, they can always cover their butts by saying, "We hired the best." The truth is, of course, there is no guaranteed best. Every project you undertake is a risk. You write a script, you see the whole thing in your head, and you hope to hell it comes out the way that you see it. Three reactions occur to me in any given scene. One. It's just the way I imagined it. Two. It's even better than I imagined it. Three. My God. What went wrong? Miscasting? The direction? The SCRIPT?

STAGE REBOUND

CHAPTER 30

At lunch one day with John, he told me about an incredible figure in the history of Haiti. A man named Henri Christophe who came to Haiti from Africa as a slave when Haiti was a French colony. Young and ambitious, Christophe set about to accomplish the impossible. Within two years, he defeated all of Napoleon's army on the island and sent them packing off to France. Establishing a monarchy with himself as king and emperor, he invited English royalty and French ambassadors to visit his kingdom. Tremendously cunning, he displayed his army to his guests by having them march in a circle around the palace in a never ending parade, making it appear that he had an army of thousands.

He built several palaces, including a mountaintop structure called the Citadel which has been compared to the Egyptian pyramids. Its ruins can still be seen today. Unfortunately, his reign eventually became tyrannical and he was assassinated by his own subjects. He remains, however, a giant figure in the black race.

The more I became immersed in researching Christophe at the New York Public Library, the more I felt Christophe would make a far more impressive subject for the stage. The months of research were a joyous necessity.

My first draft was submitted to Flora Roberts, a New York theatrical agent who represented Stephen Sondheim and several noted playwrights. She informed me that a production company called The Negro Ensemble seemed eager to do it. But then the word came that they only produced plays by "black playwrights", a bit of reverse discrimination from the past. Fortunately, Robert Kalfin, head of the Chelsea Theater Group in New York, took it on.

A cast of thirty was made possible by young actors, mostly African Americans, who were anxious to be a part of the production. The two leads were quite different in their approach to acting. James Preston, playing Christophe, was a method actor, very moody, who gradually took on the character in four weeks of rehearsal. It was a large, very difficult, demanding part, and due to his "I've got to feel it" training, there were days when I felt he simply wouldn't be up to it. On other days, he was all fire and passion and the majesty of Christophe came through in astonishing ways. The Scot's physician, played by Ed Seaman, had the part locked in early on and was all that I had hoped for.

When the Chelsea Theater Group lost their theater in Manhattan, they transferred to a just completed stage at the Brooklyn Academy of Music. Robert Kalfin, who directed as well, had his hands full during rehearsals just keeping the large cast on time and on cue everyday. I had taken a room at the Algonquin Hotel which was no larger than my tiny room on 57th Street. The trip to Brooklyn each day was sometimes difficult as taxi drivers were reluctant to go to a place where there was so much crime.

The New York Times announced the opening with a photo of James Preston and then failed to send a critic. Ditto the other New York papers except for the *Courier-Life* of Brooklyn which called it, "A brilliant choice for the opening show at the Brooklyn Academy of Music with a magnificent performance by James Preston in the lead." As a matter of fact, Preston was up for it that night but, with no money for advertising, only word of mouth kept it running for a short period.

Gordon Davidson, the managing director of the Mark Taper Forum theater in Los Angeles, read *Christophe* and contacted me in New York. He was interested in producing it for the Taper schedule, but later informed me another black play had been placed on the schedule and two black plays would be too many. He did, however, set up a luncheon appointment to meet a well-known theatrical producer, Elliot Martin, who said it had possibilities for a dramatic musical and gave the script to Leonard Bernstein. Bernstein! I waited anxiously for a month, but Bernstein eventually turned it down. That's what I was told, but I have no certainty that he ever read it. *Christophe* never rose after that. It was exhilarating, at least, to be in that theater environment again. Another ten years would go by before I'd return.

BIG SCREEN 2

CHAPTER 31

Two screenplays followed, one a supernatural story, *The Power*, in a milieu in which I don't feel comfortable, proven by lukewarm reviews. The other was an African Adventure, *The Last Safari*. The only pleasant memory I carry from that was working with Henry Hathaway again and the opportunity to witness African wildlife up-close. To see herds of wildebeest in the forest, their heads bobbing up and down from the flies invading their noses, and zebra making a black and white carpet across the savannah. On one occasion, we had a rhino charge us in an open jeep at Tsavo Park and, on another, a huge bull elephant covered in red mud at the Ngorongoro Crater took a distinct disliking to us and we cleared out quickly. As for the screenplay, the flies, if you'll excuse me, invaded my prose. The animals engendered far more life than my screenplay.

Henry invited James Stewart to see if he was interested in playing a part. I was surprised to see a very bald Stewart sans his toupee. He wasn't interested, but he did tell us a humorous story about some advice he had recently received from his business manager encouraging him to buy a large herd of goats in Texas. They were a bargain at the price. Stewart had one question for his manager. "What do you <u>do</u> with goats?" After a long silence came the reply. "I'll get right back to you, Jimmy." Stewart bought the herd and shortly afterward, the bottom fell out of the goat market.

CHAPTER 32

A tale of murder told sunny side up. That was the motif suggested in Goldman's book, *No Way to Treat a Lady*, which was written before he became one of our most successful screen writers. My adaptation departed from the story only when the book's conclusion set up a dark scene of torture and revenge.

Sol Siegel produced for Paramount and Jack Smight, who had just finished a film with Paul Newman, signed on to direct. The fine Austrian actor, Oskar Werner, who had made a name for himself in *Ship of Fools,* wanted to play the lead. He would even lower his price to play the part. As the murderer impersonates a variety of characters before he strangles his victims, from an Irish priest to a gay hairdresser to a Polish plumber, Jack and I both thought that Werner didn't have a talent for multifaceted characters. He was, however, the choice of the Paramount chief, Robert Evans. A meeting was set up with Werner which only convinced Jack and me that he was wrong for the part. Siegel wasn't certain and seemed caught in the middle.

If this dilemma wasn't enough, a deranged young actor broke into Paramount studios demanding to play the part. He was chased by studio guards through the commissary with a crowd looking on before he was caught and escorted off the lot. We thought that was the end of it, but two nights later he reappeared. Just as Siegel arrived home and stepped out of his car in the underground parking garage of his apartment building, the man approached him. With his hands held high, he claimed that he had the hands of a strangler and demanded again he play the part. Siegel told him it was Roshashana and his family was waiting for him upstairs. He agreed to see him tomorrow at his studio office. The next day, both the studio guards and the Los Angeles police were ready for the actor's arrival. This time he was arrested, kicking and screaming, and given a jail sentence. He didn't get the part.

The part, however, was still uncast. Jack said he would accept Albert Finney, but Paramount still wanted Werner. Along came Rod Steiger. He had been sent a script for the part of the second lead, a Jewish cop. An appointment was set up at Sol's apartment and Steiger arrived, insisting that he read for the part of the killer and not the cop. With Sol and me looking on, Steiger began reading several scenes. The Irish priest, the gay hairdresser, the Polish plumber all came to life. He bowled us over. Sol and I glanced at each other in each succeeding scene. My God, he was perfect.

The role of the cop then went to an actor with an engaging gift for comedy, George Segal. Jack convinced the brass to shoot entirely in New York and a two week rehearsal was scheduled in Manhattan. The delightful Lee Remick signed for the romantic lead and, joining the trio, was the diverting character actress Eileen Heckart playing Segal's Jewish mother. Heckart is Irish and there was some criticism of the choice, but I think she was faultless in the part and, after all, how many actors have played Shylock who were not Jewish?

Steiger welcomed the rehearsals and used them to full advantage, experimenting with the different ethnicities of the part. I welcomed rehearsals myself as a chance to make beneficial changes.

One evening, Jack and I had dinner with Steiger and his wife at the time, Claire Bloom. I told her that I thought Rod was an extremely versatile actor, able to play many different parts, much like Olivier. She looked at me in astonishment. "You can compare the great Olivier with Rod Steiger?" I glanced over at Steiger who was engaged, thank God, in conversation with Jack. She wasn't kidding and meant it. I knew right then that their marriage was not going to last. It didn't.

No Way to Treat a Lady opened in March of 1968. The reviews were all positive. *Variety* even reported, "Stronger direction could have pushed the film into the category of a minor classic." And, "With an excellent cast and a very good screenplay, *No Way to Treat a Lady* comes close to the quality of the best British films, notably those with Alec Guiness". The *Los Angeles Times* had the catchy banner, "A Big Hand for the Lethal Lady". Steiger got a two page article about his "stunning impersonations" in *Time* magazine. The picture made money, but it was felt a stronger box office was diminished by the tragic death of Martin Luther King, Jr., just two days before the opening.

CHAPTER 33

Westerns, as a cinematic genre, usually portrayed Indians as vicious savages. This, in spite of the fact that there were recorded incidents in which peaceful Indian villages were brutally attacked by American cavalry. Theodore Olsen wrote a very moving novel about one such assault made against the Cheyenne Indians at Wounded Knee in 1864 where women and children were massacred in a raid by Colonel Chivington and his cavalry force in spite of a flag of truce.

Ralph Nelson, who directed my Civil War *Playhouse 90* drama, secured rights to the Olsen book and contacted me to write the screenplay. He insisted upon two weeks of rehearsal before filming began. With the customary rewrites, it was sent out for casting. Word came from Candice Bergen that she wanted very much to play the feminine lead. Ralph gave her a screen test and approved of her, but I had misgivings. The part of the girl called for a hard-mouthed young woman from a tough city neighborhood and, with Candice's background of privilege, I couldn't see her in that kind of role.

Candice, Peter Strauss, Ralph, and I met at MGM and it became obvious from the first day that Candice disliked rehearsing. She didn't feel it was necessary. Her only request was to rewrite a scene where she would appear topless in a storm sequence. Her breasts, she said, were on the small side. As it turned out, the storm sequence was cut for financial reasons.

I wrote some lyrics for a tune to be sung by Donald Pleasence in the film, and the producers wanted me to supply the music as well. I composed my first, last, and only song written for a motion picture.

Soldier Blue was shot in the colonial town of San Miguel de Allende, Mexico. I didn't see the actual filming of the massacre scene or know what Ralph had done to create it. Not until the first screening of the picture. It was then I learned that amputees in Mexico were chosen for the Cheyenne villagers to make it look as though arms and legs were being cut off by cavalry swords in the battle. I found it shocking. So did many critics but, as it was based on actual fact, there were varied opinions.

"A staggeringly powerful magnificent film. Must be numbered among the most significant, brutal, liberating, and honest American films ever made. It is a movie of great art and courage." The Sunday *New York Times*.

Kevin Kelly of the *Boston Globe* said, "*Soldier Blue* is a Western of such shattering impact that remembering it now for the purpose of review is almost as overwhelming as watching it on the screen. It is the single most important film in several months."

Other reviews deplored the brutal scenes. The critic of the *Los Angeles Times*, Charles Champlin, called it "A poor excuse for the blood and guts spilling dished out."

In response came a letter to the *Times* quoting a history text used at Los Angeles colleges. "Kill and scalp all, big and little, ordered Colonel Chivington, a minister in private life. Nits make lice. The Cheyenne were scalped, had their brains knocked out. Soldiers used their knives, ripped open women, clubbed little children... mutilated their bodies in every sense of the word."

The writer of this letter was incensed that a critic could call such an event of American history "a poor excuse for violence". I know that Ralph wanted the world to know just what had happened at Wounded Knee, and he certainly accomplished that.

The picture was far more popular in Europe than it was here. In fact, it had higher grosses in Italy than any other picture that year. The incredible thing is that, in Italy, it was considered a love story and a woman's picture. It played for weeks in London and other cities, and Ralph toured the world to promote the film from Bombay to Bangkok.

Today, I still have serious misgivings about Ralph using amputees in the violent scenes. There was, however, only one area of censorship thrust upon us in the making of the film. At several points, the girl refers to the soldier's defense of the cavalry as "bullshit". We had to cut it. Candice would only be allowed to say "bull".

CHAPTER 34

Bobbie and I were on summer vacation when I got a call to come back to Los Angeles. Something important had come up. Swannie had a call from Paul Newman's production company. They wanted me to meet Newman to discuss a book which turned out to be a stunning epic novel, a story of an Oregon lumber family with deeply human characters in a story. The problem would be bringing the plots and subplots to a two-hour screenplay.

I met Newman at the Los Angeles Forum packed with people gathered there not as sports fans, but extras paid to be in the picture *WUSA* starring Newman. And there he was, in character as I arrived, standing up on a platform addressing the crowd. I was intimidated even before I met him.

I was directed to a small dressing room in the rear. We sat facing each other on canvas chairs to discuss the novel. I told him my initial reaction to the book, the characters, and the structure. I spoke of areas I'd consider eliminating and still not lose what I thought to be the power of Kesey's work. More than anything, I said how much I admired the book. That part was easy.

Newman, at this first meeting, appeared to agree with my ideas. In fact, he was ready to sign me immediately and wanted my payment to be a percentage of the profits. Agents call that a percentage of nothing if there's no front money. Studio accountants see to it the picture never makes a profit. It seemed unusual for the star of the picture to bring up contract negotiations.

Fortunately, John Foreman dissuaded him before it became an issue. Swannie gave Universal my price. They were shocked by it. That's standard, too. Always be shocked first as a bargaining point to begin negotiations. I stayed out of it and let the agents do their work.

The first few days, working out of Newman's dressing room at Paramount, I made an outline of the six hundred-odd pages, breaking it down once again to the essentials. Newman and I had occasional discussions as I proceeded, but I found him non-committal most of the time. John Foreman, however, the producer of the film, was completely accessible and very receptive to my ideas.

At my request, Foreman arranged a helicopter trip over the Oregon woods to see how a lumber company operated. I flew over several camps and watched the strenuous, sometimes dangerous life of loggers. It was all that Kesey had said it was. Back home again, I tackled the screenplay and, by January, I gave both Newman and Foreman a complete script. Newman asked me back to his home in Connecticut for a script conference.

A charming rustic farmhouse in a wooded area of Westport came into view as I approached. First thing I noticed was a trampoline in the side yard for the children. I met Paul's wife, Joanne Woodward, who was very gracious considering that her husband had unexpectedly invited me to dinner. Seated around a table in a delightful country dining room, we sipped generous martinis which Paul had prepared with black olives. We chatted without mention of the script and then Paul, in a spontaneous gesture, asked me to stay overnight at a guest house he owned nearby. No pajamas. No toothbrush. I accepted, of course.

The next morning, more script discussions while Paul drove me around in his souped up Volkswagen. Once in awhile, he would burst out of an intersection astonishing other drivers at the power of the little bug.

We had a final lunch in New York the following week at a mid-town Japanese restaurant. Marlon Brando and John Foreman joined us in a private room. Newman and Brando both abhorred being seen in public, understandable since they couldn't go anywhere in the world without being recognized. Two days later, at Sardi's restaurant, Rod Steiger was less disturbed by an admiring public.

He strode across the room to greet me with outstretched arms, surprisingly open, convivial, warm, and friendly, saying how proud he was of *No Way to Treat a Lady*. Not the self-centered Rod I was used to. With outstretched arms he said how proud he was of *No Way to Treat a Lady*. Such largess from Rod caught me off guard. A dedicated actor, but rarely a sociable fellow.

Returning home, I resumed the rewrites. I also remained active in the Writers Guild, elected to the Guild Board. I eventually served on the Producer-Writers Health-Pension Fund and the Guild Negotiating Committee, securing benefits for writers. I even worked for the Guild's Credit Union, which was unusual considering my abysmal grasp of mathematics.

In my office at Paramount one morning, I heard Paul's voice in the production office next door. He was speaking favorably about my second draft. I soon discovered it wasn't Paul Newman's voice. It belonged to his brother, Arthur, who had the same indistinguishable tone and speech pattern. Arthur was working as a production manger on the picture. I was pleased that he liked the script but even more pleased later that day when I found out that his brother, Paul, liked it. It was a go.

A location for the film had to be found. The novel called for a house by a river which was central to the story. John Foreman, Arthur Newman, and I, along with two production assistants, boarded a Lear jet out of Burbank airport to scout places along the Pacific Coast. Jet planes require two pilots and one of the two on the field looked to me like a college kid, while the other appeared to be a seasoned aviator. As it turned out, the kid was the one in the pilot's seat. He turned out to be John Lear, the son of Bill Lear, creator of the popular Lear jet. Born to it, John Lear had been flying all his life. I learned he had once flown illegally under the Golden Gate Bridge. Skilled. But reckless? I'd soon find out.

On our way to Northern California, John executed several barrel rolls. To my surprise, I found that there was no sensation other than seeing the sky through the window roll to land and the land to sky and back again three times. The coffee at my side never budged. Not a drop spilled. Another maneuver, however, <u>did</u> turn my stomach. John would bring the jet down to a height only a few hundred feet above the ground and look for a suitable house by a river. Unsuccessful, Foreman would say, "Nothing here. Take her up!" I don't know what G force came about, but I felt as though we were suddenly in an astronaut's centrifuge. This maneuver was repeated many times over California, Oregon, Washington, and British Columbia. I never got used to it. And we never found a house matching the one described in the book.

We did, however, find a river in Oregon which was very much like the one in the novel and made the decision to build a house there. The property owners were paid for the use of their land with a choice of keeping the house (no electricity or plumbing) or having the studio tear it down, leaving everything just as it was. They decided to keep the house, and it's still there today on the Siletz River.

A search for a director began. George Roy Hill wasn't interested. Joseph Manckewitz suggested changes with no commitment to direct. Newman-Foreman looked for a director. Then the roof caved in.

Newman-Foreman and Universal couldn't agree on a contract. It was over. Disappointed, I went off to Palm Desert with the family to try and put the whole thing out of my mind. It was a rather depressing attempt, but it ended with a pleasant surprise. Somehow, a deal had been made. The picture was on again.

CHAPTER 35

Filming began for *Sometimes A Great Notion* on June 15th with a young new director, Richard Colla. Henry Fonda was the first choice for the patriarch of the family and I was thrilled when he accepted. We were also fortunate to cast Lee Remick as Newman's wife. This would be my third picture with her, and I told Foreman it was the best choice he could have made. Gene Hackman was brought in to discuss the part of Newman's brother, Joby, and I hoped he'd take it. He didn't get the chance. As it turned out, Paul gave the part to Richard Jaeckel. Michael Sarrazin completed the cast as Newman's son.

They wanted me on location in Oregon for the entire shoot. Seated next to Sarrazin on the plane, I told him how much I admired his film, *They Shoot Horses Don't They?* He seemed entirely disinterested, if not annoyed, and I didn't pursue the matter. In fact, Sarrazin was so non-communicative, we rarely talked during the filming of the picture. We landed in Portland where we were met by a company car and driven to Salishan, a luxurious resort community on the ocean. I stayed there for a week or two until the family joined me at a beach cottage the company had rented for us just a mile away, right on the sand.

The anticipated moment of the first reading had finally arrived. Every actor in every major part gathered around the table in a large conference room at the resort. Then, it began. Although Paul had approved the script, he interrupted the reading constantly and started ripping it apart. To my astonishment, it was a sort of general mauling of scenes we had gone over together so many times. I looked over at Fonda who seemed unsettled at Paul's behavior. I had the feeling Fonda didn't want to change anything. We read steadily, though, until one p.m., broke off for the afternoon, and resumed at seven that evening.

Paul continued to tear it apart. When he left the room for a moment, Fonda said he was appalled at the changes "that gentleman", meaning Newman, wanted now. Fonda said he signed on to do the picture because he liked the script. <u>This</u> script. "Does the gentleman <u>want</u> to do this picture?"

When the day of acrimony was over, I took off immediately, with voluminous notes, to my Royal portable typewriter to see if I could make some sense out of what presently bothered Newman. I typed all night until dawn, going over every scene in the entire script. Foreman was at breakfast in his office the next morning when I staggered in with the results. I figured I'd be on my way back home shortly. Late that afternoon, there came an unbelievable response. Foreman called to tell me that he and Paul had read the changes. They loved them. Loved them?

Rehearsals were held at a local high school and Paul became more accessible. In fact, he said that it had been pretty rough for me, and he was sorry about that, and he'd like to send me a case of my favorite booze. I told him to forget it. He did.

Fonda was an actor who came from the theater. This became evident on the first day of shooting in a scene where striking lumbermen curse at the Stamper family from across the river and the Stampers respond in kind. I gave the cast a few angry lines for the family to shout and encouraged them to add their own. Not Fonda. He wanted me to write each and every line. No improvisation for him. No changing of lines. Actors are not writers. Unlike some film actors, he adhered scrupulously to every word in the script. With someone as dedicated to his craft as Fonda, trained in the theater, every line becomes the truth. He was incapable of "acting".

We celebrated the first day of filming with a party on the beach at sunset.

Foreman barbecued the steaks, Fonda prepared a batch of his homemade ice cream, and Foreman's wife, Linda Lawson, who had a part in the picture, tossed the salad. And so we began with the usual ups and downs, the good days and the difficult days. Some things worked and some things didn't. The one person who wasn't working out, however, was the director, Richard Colla, whom Paul had personally chosen. Fonda was unhappy with his directing style. But I was pleased with the rushes I had seen. I thought the camera work was very inventive, and the actors were all that I had hoped for.

For almost a week, the decision had been made to let Richard go even though he hadn't been told. I assumed that Newman must have felt the same way about him as Fonda did. It was a terrible situation. Everyone seemed to know except Richard himself. At any rate, he left at the end of the second week. Who would take over at this stage? Newman had directed before, a highly praised film with his wife, Joanne, called *Rachel, Rachel*. It wasn't a difficult decision for Paul as I think he looked forward to directing again. In fact, he took over almost immediately.

During the filming, various friends of the Newmans came to visit. As I walked into the lobby of the Salishan Resort one day, I saw Marlon Brando standing there, chatting with Foreman. Brando stared at me intently. "What have you been on? Your eyes. My God."

I didn't know what the hell he was talking about and hastened to the men's room at the first opportunity to look in the mirror. Nothing. Foreman told me later that he loved to play pranks on people.

That night, Paul wanted to show Marlon what his new Corvette could do on the highway. As Paul had already downed a few belts of scotch, we were all concerned, especially Joanne. But to everyone's relief, they returned within the hour, Marlon looking pale and haggard. I was told later that Marlon had played another prank. When Paul's eyes were on the road, Marlon secretly turned off the ignition, stopping the car, and then took over the wheel.

Weeks later, Brando's agents contacted me to write a screenplay about the Native American Indian. It turned out he had loved *Soldier Blue* as it championed the Indian cause. There was no real commitment to the project, however, and the idea passed away quietly.

The irrepressible actress, Cloris Leachman, arrived with her children for a few days, as did Shirley MacLaine, both very good friends of the Newmans. They joined our family for cookouts on the beach in front of our cottage by moonlight. Soon after they left Salishan, the Gilroys arrived, and Frank brought along a new screenplay he had written called *Dangerous Characters*, from a novel by Paula Fox. I read it, saw an intriguing part for Shirley MacLaine, and gave it to Foreman who agreed with me. When I asked Frank for permission to give it to MacLaine, he said he didn't think she was right for it.

"Let her, at least, read it," I said. With his permission, I gave her the screenplay with no offer attached, and she loved it. She and Frank met a few weeks later, a contract was worked out, and Frank directed her in it that fall in New York. The film went on to win the top prize at the Berlin Film Festival.

Georgia Pacific, a paper company in Oregon, was hosting an opening reception for a new high rise building in Portland. The governor would be there with many dignitaries, and they asked us to attend. Newman would never face a public gathering such as this, and Sarrazin declined. Fonda, Jaeckel (Jake), and I were picked up and flown to Portland in a private Georgia Pacific plane and then whisked off to a hotel across the street from the new building. Tuxedos were provided and we joined the crowd, starting on the top floor and working our way down, one floor at a time. Champagne flowed for three floors until Fonda, partial to Jack Daniels sour mash, wondered if there was anything but champagne. From that floor on, bourbon was supplied to Fonda until we reached the lobby. He was so swacked by then that Jake and I could hardly believe he was still vertical and moving.

The Governor of Oregon, Tom McCall, and the three of us were expected to give a speech. Jake and I couldn't see how Fonda could manage it. But damned if he didn't come through with an amusing speech geared to the people of Oregon. We returned to the hotel, got out of our tuxedos, and Fonda slept on the plane all the way back to the location. Since I lived in the cottage next to Fonda on the beach, Jake suggested that I drive Fonda home as Fonda was in no condition to drive himself. I brought him to his door and saw that he got in all right. Arriving at my place, I realized I hadn't brought my key. I didn't want to wake up the family, so I jumped up and through an open window, bruising a rib so badly that I had to wear binding around it for the next two weeks.

The next morning, we spoke to Fonda about his speech the night before. He didn't remember a word of it. Worse, he didn't even remember that he gave a speech. In fact, he said he didn't remember much of anything after the fourteenth floor.

CHAPTER 36

A crisis. Paul fell from a motorcycle while preparing a bike racing scene on a circular dirt track. It meant a delay in production and Paul on crutches for ten days.

When we resumed filming, an actor was needed for a five line part to play a doctor in a scene with Henry. Due to the expense of sending for an actor from Hollywood, they took the cheaper way out. John Gay. As we drove to the local hospital where the filming would take place, Henry suggested we go over the scene together. I welcomed the opportunity, but soon discovered that he just wanted someone to cue him.

After the scene was shot, still dressed in character as a doctor, I happened to pause by the maternity room to glance through a window at three newly born infants. The two women standing next to me assumed I had delivered them. I smiled and moved on. Why not? As for my brilliant acting tour de force, the scene was chopped in half. Perhaps Fonda wasn't good enough?

The director, George Roy Hill, came by to visit our set and offered some suggestions about the filming. We spoke of the early days of television and when he directed my teleplay, *The Devil as a Roaring Lion*, some fifteen years ago. He told me for the first time that he liked the play and wondered where I got the idea of the boy and the suspected murderer. I really didn't know. Some plays arrive on gossamer wings and you're never quite sure where they came from. We also recalled how the child actor in the play forgot the line from the scripture that became the very title of the play. Live TV. Those were the days.

In the same restaurant at the resort two days later, Paul, Joanne, Fonda, Hill, and I were having lunch. Paul, as usual, sat with his back to the room so as not to be recognized. A woman spotted him, however, and approached us with a menu in hand. She wanted Paul's signature for her daughter, Nancy. Paul explained that we were having lunch now, but if she notified the studio, they would send her an autographed photo with her daughter's name on it. With that, he thought, she'd go away. As she started to leave, miffed, she suddenly recognized Fonda.

"Mr. Fonda! I didn't see you there! Would you please sign this menu for my daughter, Nancy?"

Henry turned on the charm. "I'd love to." He took the menu from her, wrote down something, and then handed it to Hill, who grinned, a huge wide grin before handing it to Joanne. She, too, smiled and shook her head, handing it to me. I couldn't quite believe what I saw and gave it to Paul who burst out laughing before handing it back to the woman. The note said, "Dear Nancy. Paul Newman is a shit." It was signed Henry Fonda. The woman walked off without even looking at it. What a surprise for her daughter.

Rushes were shown at a local movie theater in a small paper mill town near Salishan. It had a glassed off area for mothers with screaming babies, an advantage that some larger theaters are employing today.

Paul, Fonda, John Foreman, and I stood talking to the theater manager who wore a T-shirt emblazoned with the name of the film he was showing that week. "What," asked Foreman "was the biggest hit you ever had here?"

"Without any question," said the theater manager, "The Love Bug." He said they could have held it over for another two weeks, but the Disney Company wouldn't let him. Fonda then asked him how the film *They Shoot Horses, Don't They?* fared in his theater since it starred Fonda's daughter, Jane.

"Mr. Fonda. I couldn't get a horse in to see that picture!"

Henry smiled. In fact, we all had a laugh.

My family returned home before the film was completed to see Malibu ablaze with hillside fires in a September eat wave. It quickly burned out. I left Oregon before the final day's filming and missed the wrap party. Post-production lay ahead.

In Los Angeles, Paul took over the editing of the film. He called one day to show me a juxtaposition of scenes he had made near the beginning of the film, placing a showdown with the lumberman's union before the appearance of Michael Sarrazin. A big change, and I didn't like it as it brought in the union conflict too soon but, as Paul once said, "The success or failure of the film will be my responsibility. All decisions will be made by me." And so they were.

Another discussion took place at the Beverly Hills hotel. Paul and I were walking across a broad lawn, deep in conversation, when we saw someone approaching us from a bungalow. Richard Burton. He had just had a roaring quarrel with Elizabeth Taylor and wanted Paul to smooth things over. Paul looked very uncomfortable. I don't know what happened as I thought it best to leave.

Henry Mancini was busy composing the film's score and a song for the opening of the picture. We'd previously talked about using *Goodnight Irene* for the title sequence as it gave the title to the book. "Sometimes I live in the country. Sometimes I live in the town. Sometimes I take a great notion to jump in the river and drown. Irene, goodnight…" Without it, audiences would wonder where the title originated. Newman said it didn't matter. He had acted in a film called *Somebody Up There Likes Me* and claimed that nobody knew what that title meant either. Our opening song became Mancini's song, *All My Children*, but the film's title remained. In Europe, however, it became *Never Give An Inch*, the Stamper family motto. Actually, it made more sense.

The picture opened in '71 to mixed reviews. Most of the criticism came from adapting a screenplay from such a lengthy epic novel. I certainly agreed with that. But under the circumstances and, God, there were plenty of them, I think it came out damn well. I had been apprehensive about casting Richard Jaeckel. As it turned out, he was the only actor to receive an Academy Award nomination. Both Newman and Foreman were pleased with the film, and there were enough good reviews, along with a strong box office, to make the execs at Universal happy. All in all, it certainly made for a memorable summer on the coast of Oregon.

CHAPTER 37

One dark, drizzly January morning, my brother called me to say that Mom had passed away in her sleep. It was totally unexpected and the sudden realization was hard to accept. Jim and I were grateful, at least, that she died peacefully without suffering a protracted illness.

Mom had requested to have her organs donated to research at USC. We stood in front of her mobile home and watched, in tears, as they placed her body on a stretcher into a station wagon. A station wagon. It seemed so inappropriate. So indecent. We kept on watching as it moved off the mobile lot and disappeared down the street. She was gone. Just like that.

Mom, of course, had lived a long full life. Sadly, it wasn't much later that Rod Serling passed away from complications arising from a coronary by-pass. He was only fifty. My age. We were shocked, of course, and for Carol and the children, an excruciating difficult period. Our two families had spent many weekend vacations together and the loss affected all of us.

The Writers Guild of America felt it was now past the time to increase minimum wages and health and retirement benefits. A strike was finally called against the major studios. Films already in production would be finished, but no rewriting would be allowed and no scripts would be purchased. Picket lines became my thrice weekly activity, along with manning the Guild's hot line to answer questions from the members. Writers from all of the English speaking countries observed our strike and refused to work until it was settled. The weeks became months.

When the strike finally concluded, an independent film company, American International Pictures, sent me a manuscript, *Hennessy*, about an Irish architect whose wife and child are killed on a city street before his eyes during the crossfire of British troops and Irish insurgents. The script told of Hennessy's almost maniacal revenge as he makes his way to London to assassinate Queen Elizabeth of England. A very provocative premise and I didn't want the characters to be overwhelmed by the plot.

A British director, John Guillerman, signed on, and I flew to London to confer with British Lion Company brought in as co-producer. Then we took three more quick round trips to London before the script was approved. Guillerman didn't mind; he'd been a British fighter pilot in World War II and loved flying. I wish I could say the same.

Still another trip was made to Italy to interview Rod Steiger who was filming *The Last Days of Benito Mussolini* in the title role. He came striding into the lobby of his hotel in full makeup from the set. One would swear that Il Duce himself had come back to life. Guillerman and I told him the story of *Hennessy* over several glasses of wine in the lounge and he seemed receptive but made no commitment. Actors always conferred with their agents first as to payment for the part and how long the commitment will last. A few days later, he signed up.

As it turned out, Guillerman did not direct the picture. He received an offer to direct *The Towering Inferno* with Paul Newman and Steve McQueen and was wanted immediately. *Hennessy* was without a director for two months before Don Sharp, a talented director in London, took over the helm. I knew Sharp's work, respected him, and was pleased that he was enthusiastic about the script. My expectations for the project increased even more when my favorite actress, Lee Remick, was signed to play opposite Steiger.

The fifth of November in England is called Guy Fawkes Day, commemorating the gunpowder plot to blow up the House of Lords in 1604. It's a day set aside each year for the Queen of England to address the full Parliament. Fox Newsreel had actual footage of the ceremony with Elizabeth II which Sharp intercut with the fictional footage, just as Steiger is set to explode a bomb strapped to his chest. In one moment of the newsreel footage, the Queen looks up from her prepared speech, distracted by something. Cut to Steiger, just about to detonate the explosive when a Scotland Yard detective stops him. Steiger escapes, running out to the garden outside the Parliament building, only to be killed as bullets strike him and the bomb explodes.

The scene was shocking to British censors and created extensive controversy. So much so that the government banned it from the first run theater in Lester Square after a week. With subsequent screenings in England and elsewhere, however, the film was successful financially. I don't believe the picture would be made today in view of the proliferation of suicide bombings. At least not with actual Fox newsreel footage.

CHAPTER 38

Vincente Minnelli had always wanted to direct a picture starring his daughter, Liza. He found a novel, *Film of Memory*, by Maurice Druon, set in 1920s Rome about a hotel chambermaid, Carmela, who learns about life and love from an aging Countess. Not the usual sort of fare for a commercial movie. Minnelli was anxious to do it, however, and we met a few times to explore the possibilities without any contract obligations. Keen interest from American International Pictures (AIP), the production company that produced *Hennessy*, made our decision to go ahead with *Film of Memory*.

Vincente went off to Rome for pre-production work after conferring with me over my first draft. Three weeks later, I followed him and stopped in New York on the way to see Liza who was appearing for a limited time as a replacement in the musical *Chicago*. Backstage after the show, I voiced my concerns about AIP. Having worked with AIP before, I knew them to be aggressively independent and difficult. I told Liza that I hoped Vincente would be up to the task of working with them. She assured me that although Vincente had a soft way of speaking, he was tough as nails when it came to dealing with producers. After all, he'd been doing it all his life.

In Rome, I conferred with Vincente again at the studio. When Liza arrived at the end of the month, she, Vincente, and I spent one whole evening going over the script until four in the morning. Liza read her part, I read the rest, and Vincente listened. Acting again. A magical evening. But the harmony wouldn't last.

Ingrid Bergman arrived to play the role of the Countess and let it be known that she didn't think she was right for the part. I could think of no one else who would have been better.

It was decided by the producers that the film should have a song, performed by Liza, for the opening and closing titles. The Broadway musical team, Kander and Ebb, friends of Liza's, composed it, and the song then became the title of the picture, *A Matter of Time*. The team had written memorable musicals, *Cabaret, Chicago, Zorba* and others, but I couldn't help but think their music, this time, sounded too contemporary for the period of the story.

Once filming began, Liza, who had been very cooperative before, was uptight and complained about everything from her hairdresser to the line producer. The fact that her last picture, *Lucky Lady*, received bad reviews didn't help matters. I was slowly beginning to get negative feelings as I headed back home.

My feelings were confirmed when a call came for me to come back to Rome immediately. Minnelli and the producers were barely speaking to each other. Déjà vu. I was called to bring about a reconciliation as I had once before between Minnelli and Julian Blaustein during *The Four Horsemen of the Apocalypse*. This time, the breach was even wider. AIP wanted new scenes edited out of chronological context which would change the ending and bring it to what I thought would be an improbable conclusion. Vincente shared my feelings. A compromise was made and I was led to believe, erroneously, that AIP accepted it and would not pursue any more changes.

On the set one day, I watched a very dramatic scene between Liza and Ingrid Bergman. Liza had asked me to observe her performance and I did. However, Bergman was so extraordinary, so moving in the scene, that when it was over I spoke to Bergman immediately. Big mistake. When I turned to Liza, I could see anger and disappointment. I insisted she was just fine and I meant it. My approval came too late. I don't think she ever quite forgave me for speaking to Bergman first.

Back home again, I was told that Vincente was increasingly pressured by Sam Arkoff of AIP. They were wearing him down with negative comments. Liza had told me in New York, "Daddy's never intimidated by producers, he has nerves of steel." Perhaps. But this time the production company took the editing away from Vincente and made the final cut. The result was disastrous.

Word soon came out about AIP's shabby treatment of Minnelli. Thirty leading directors, from Sidney Lumet to Martin Scorsese to Frank Capra, wrote a declaration published in the trades. "Vincente Minnelli's latest film, *A Matter of Time,* is being released to the public and critics in a re-edited, revised, altered and distorted form that has nothing whatever to do with his original concept. We register a strong and urgent protest."

The picture turned out to be Minnelli's last film. I wondered later if the experience in Rome had anything to do with the slow developing dementia, Alzheimer's, which struck him later in life, similar to Rita Hayworth. I remembered how he had seemed distracted and vague in his responses. I visited him many times at his home in Beverly Hills after *A Matter of Time* and witnessed his slow withdrawal from life, his mind always straying, unable to finish sentences. To my amazement, a party was held at his house one night with many actors, producers, and directors. Vincente sat in a robe with everyone around him and didn't recognize a soul.

The private funeral service was held in a small chapel at Forest Lawn Mortuary in 1986. I felt privileged to be invited along with his close friends. Vincente's wife, Lee Anderson, sat across the aisle from me next to Michael Jackson and a tearful Liza. In a row behind them were James Stewart and Bob Hope. Eulogies were made by Gregory Peck and Kirk Douglas whom I would see again at a much later date under quite different circumstances. When the gathering passed the open casket, I looked down at Vincente in his ever-present yellow jacket and black trousers. He had always treated me with such respect, and I realized at that moment how very much I was going to miss him.

CHAPTER 39

A call from Renée Valente, a very shrewd, engaging casting director turned producer. "Frank Sinatra is interested in doing a feature film of his life." Renée, a good friend of Sinatra's, wondered if I'd be interested in talking to him about it. Actually, I was and I wasn't. I was hugely attracted to the possibilities, but I was nervous about meeting the Mount Everest of the entertainment industry. His turbulent life and career involved prominent political leaders, many women, and associations with the Mafia. Daunting, yes, but at least I could explore the possibilities.

Renée set up an interview and we met at the Sam Goldwyn Studios where he kept a very comfortable wood paneled office in a bungalow on the lot and greeted me in shirt and slacks, looking every inch the debonair Frank Sinatra, friendly and outgoing. I told him that so much of the material I had read about his life seemed to be bogus gossip column fodder and a few obvious hatchet jobs. I said I'd be very interested if we could create a truthful portrayal from events in his life, good and bad, as only he knew them to be. He seemed very agreeable and invited me and Renée to his home in the Palm Springs area.

Driving through the gates, we saw a large walled compound. The main house itself, just ahead of us, was comparatively small, while a separate studio to our left, we discovered, was large enough inside to serve as a ballroom. We had also heard that his office had a model train with lights and whistles which circled around the room near the ceiling. Renée and I were given separate suites in the guest quarters where Prince Charles and Princess Diana had once stayed.

The taping began after lunch on a deck outside the studio. I wanted to review the early days first and discovered that Sinatra had a photographic memory of events and could describe the physical appearance of people, places, and objects. In one incident, he talked of a meeting with his father, a fireman, at his station in Hoboken and could describe the old brick structure of the firehouse and the very clothes his father was wearing that day. It was early in Frank's career and publicity was beginning to circulate about him. His father had never wanted him to be a nightclub singer since he didn't consider it a real job. With this rift between them, the old man looked at his son facing him at the opposite end of the firehouse, and suddenly slammed shut a locker door as though he was hiding something.

"What's in there?" Frank asked.

His father reluctantly opened the door to reveal a publicity photo of Sinatra taped inside. It was an awkward moment for the old man.

We taped throughout the afternoon and quit about five o'clock. Sinatra said he had a few people coming over for dinner in an hour or so. Very informal. No need to change. Renée said to me, "I don't know about you, but I'm not taking any chances. I'm changing."

We returned to the main house two hours later, having both showered and changed, and looked through the window to see a dozen people milling about the bar. The moment we walked in, someone immediately bumped into me, accidentally spilling his drink on my jacket. He apologized, saying, "Sorry. I'm Ted Agnew. How do you do?" I was surprised to suddenly see Spiro Agnew, the former Vice President under Nixon, a man who'd been forced out of office because of fraudulent dealings when he was Governor of Maryland. He and his wife were now the Sinatra's neighbors, living in Palm Springs. Renée and I were seated with them and Sinatra at one of the three small tables in the dining room which Sinatra, kidding, called the "A" table.

The party was over about eleven and after the guests had left, Sinatra invited Renée and me over to his studio. Bourbon on the rocks was offered, and

I nursed one glass for the next three hours while we listened to some recent recordings of his in progress. In the early hours of the morning, Renée and I left. Sinatra was still sipping bourbon.

The next morning, 8 a.m., and Frank was already there, ready to tape, showing no signs of staying up late. We moved on to the area of his early nightclub engagements and the shady characters who owned them. The word "Mafia" wasn't mentioned, but Frank, indicating them, would make a gesture of bending his nose to one side. We worked steadily until lunch and then continued on all afternoon. Eventually, we hit a wall. The women. Obviously there were many women in his life, but he wouldn't talk about them. "Not now. We'll get into that later."

That night, he and Barbara invited me and Renée to a party he threw at a local restaurant for several leading professional golfers and their wives. It broke up late but, once again the next morning, bright and early, Frank was eager to talk again about his early life and his breakthrough to stardom on the stage of the Paramount Theater. One important element was still missing. He avoided information about the women in his life. And this was the last day of taping. When would he open up? "Later," he kept saying. I was getting the feeling now that he might never be ready to talk about them.

In the evening, Sinatra and I watched a solo performance of Pavarotti on television while Barbara and Renée went off to see a movie in the screening room. We were sitting there in the living room watching the tube when he said, "Look at Pavarotti's collar." I saw nothing unusual. "His collar...loose around the neck. Gives him full diaphragmatic control." Ever since that time, I've noticed other opera singers. Sinatra was right, of course.

Not much later, he announced that he wasn't feeling well and said he'd take penicillin and go to bed. We said goodnight. I never saw him when we left the next morning. Renée and I were both disappointed that he never got around to talking about his women, but she said to let it ride for now. He'll come around. But he didn't. Not with me, at least.

A year or so later, Renée called to tell me that they were now considering several writers for the Sinatra story and I would be one of them. I talked it over with her and politely declined.

ON STAGE!

CHAPTER 40

There had been only a few one-person plays and the idea of writing one always intrigued me. Because of my experience playing in *The Importance of Being Earnest* at Boothbay, my first thought was of Oscar Wilde. A genius of wit and amusement. He not only had both of those attributes, but there was great theatrical drama in a life destroyed by the notoriety of homosexuality. He once identified himself in his own words as the man who "awakened the imagination of my century." Plays, poems, novels, stories, and essays were there to draw upon. I called the play *Well Chosen Enemies* from a Wilde line about the importance of knowing your enemies.

The one technique I did not want to employ was creating scenes with Wilde speaking to imaginary people and using imaginary props. I placed him in a time after his trial for sodomy, subsequent imprisonment, and eventual exile to Paris. Penniless, a notorious figure, I put him on a concert hall stage where he could speak directly to a Parisian audience. Wilde's income would enable him not only to rent the hall, but to keep him in his Paris apartment for a few more weeks.

In the first act, I envisioned his manner light and amusing, giving Wilde the opportunity to make comments about life and art. In the second act, he becomes a figure of tragedy brought down by his lover, Lord Alfred Douglas. Using Wilde's own words, he speaks to the audience with passion, but also with that ever-present wit which never failed him.

I became so engrossed with the project that for several months I worked all day and into the evening, enjoying every moment of it. Then came the usual problem. How to proceed? David Rintels, an excellent skilled writer, had written a fine, celebrated one-man play about the famous lawyer, Clarence Darrow, which had starred Henry Fonda. David put me in touch with the theatrical law firm, Loeb and Loeb, who notified me within two weeks they had two producers, Mike Wise and Frank Levy, ready to mount a production with Vincent Price as Wilde, directed by Joseph Hardy. Price, of course, was well-known for his many portrayals in horror films, but I also knew of his acclaimed work in the theater. It began in his early twenties, in London, playing opposite Helen Hayes, Broadway's leading lady, in *Queen Victoria*. A most auspicious debut.

One huge hurdle for Price was the challenge in memorizing a script that called for him to be on stage alone for almost two hours. The play was rehearsed at a stage on the 20th Century Fox Studio lot, with Joseph Hardy directing, where I was invited to see what they had accomplished. Filled with anxiety and some apprehension, I watched Price disappear and become Wilde. All that I had hoped for. The play was left as written with one exception. Hardy didn't like my title, *Well Chosen Enemies,* and suggested *Diversions and Delights.* The more I thought about it, the better I liked it.

The opening performance in San Francisco was at the Marines Memorial Theater in July of 1977. My family joined me for the occasion, and we sat with our eyes glued to the stage as Price strolled out, wearing an auburn wig and period costume, a yellow rose in his hand. He took the stage and commanded it for the entire evening. The laughter from the audience in the first act was followed by sober silence in the second when Wilde was sentenced to prison for sodomy. I said to myself, "It's working. It *is* working. He's got them." When it was over, he strolled off the stage just as he had strolled on. The curtain call brought a standing ovation. Price, amidst the applause, threw the yellow rose to the audience. It was a gesture he repeated from then on at every performance.

Chapter Forty

All three local papers were beyond my most optimistic expectations. "It's an utter spellbinder," said the *San Francisco Examiner.* "Profound and moving," said the *San Francisco Chronicle.* And, during the run, it broke all box office records at the Marines Memorial Theater. Promising to be sure, but perhaps San Francisco's large gay population was responsible for the play's success.

While it was booked in San Francisco, other cities were now lined up for a tour. In Chicago, Baltimore, and Washington D.C., audiences proved to be just as rewarding. I hailed a cab in Washington to the historic Ford's Theater where Lincoln was killed. Much to my amazement, the driver, an African American, didn't know where it was located. I gave him directions and, when we arrived, I mentioned the Lincoln assassination. He became animated and excited. "Here? You sayin' Lincoln was killed right here?" I assured him that he was and pointed to the building across the street where Lincoln was taken for a time before he died.

There was a long silence. The driver just stood there staring at the building. He was still gazing at it when I paid him. Just before I entered the theater, I looked back to see him standing by his taxi, shaking his head in wonder.

Washington D.C. had changed in some ways from the time I had lived there in 1942. The old coffee shop that I frequented every morning before work was now part of a medical building. The streetcar line no longer existed. And little did I ever think I'd have a play opening there at the Ford Theater. Tempus fugit.

Our next stop, Boston, was known as a tryout town for obvious reasons. Many plays and musicals have opened there before going on to Broadway and many have died there, too. Boston had two renowned critics who could kill a play with a bad review before it even got to New York. The theater was full as Price strolled out on the stage once again and took the audience deftly into the palm of his hand.

The next morning, fingers crossed, I grabbed Elliot Norton's review in the *Boston Herald American.* "If we are to have one person plays, let them all be witty, wise, and charming like *Diversions and Delights.*" And from Kevin

Kelley, the *Boston Globe* critic, "John Gay has struck both an indelible portrait and a memorable if miniature drama...richly and wonderfully funny." Vincent was delighted, of course, and God knows I was, too. It sounded like a winner, but Boston isn't New York. Nothing could have prepared us for what happened.

At the opening night performance at the Eugene O'Neill Theater in Manhattan, I stood in the back the entire time and watched with such anxiety that I might as well have been on stage myself. Vincent seemed to be just a little on edge in the first few moments, but then took control. If the reviews should prove negative, I felt it couldn't be from his performance. The audience, as in other theaters, gave him an ovation at the final curtain.

Heartened by the reception, we went off to a party provided by the producers at Sardis, the famous theatrical restaurant. Several celebs were there whom I had never met, including Christopher Buckley, son of William Buckley, the noted conservative writer. Christopher had published an article in *Esquire* magazine praising Vincent Price as Oscar Wilde without mention of John Gay. Here was an unexpected opportunity to point that out to him in somewhat blunt terms. He didn't respond.

Such parties at Sardis are a tradition in the theater. They can be exhilarating or painful, depending on the reaction of the critics. Bobbie and I sat with the Gilroys and waited to hear the first television reviews. Both good. The most important review came from the morning's edition of *The New York Times*. Richard Eder praised Vincent's performance as touching and delicate...but then went on to criticize the play. "The material fights the dramatic framework." He thought the amusing first act weakened and undermined the dramatic monologue of the second act. I couldn't have disagreed with him more. It's the contrast of the two acts that make it work. In New York, however, the prestigious *The New York Times* can make or break a play. The other reviews the next morning helped, at least, to ease the pain.

Both *Time* and *Newsweek* good. "Gay has woven Wilde's work into a vigorous portrait," *The New Yorker*. Clive Barnes of the *New York Post* found it,

"Witty, amusing and, at times, moving." The irony is that, at one time, Barnes was the critic for *The New York Times*. If he had still been there, the prospects of *Diversions and Delights* in New York might have been different. I wouldn't want to give the impression there were no bad reviews. There was one. Deadly. The *Women's Wear Daily.* "If Wilde wasn't dull, Vincent Price is."

I stayed in New York during the short run, visiting backstage with Price at every performance. I still treasure a letter he wrote me later, sharing the disappointment of the Broadway opening.

At a matinee one day, he came in an hour early to speak to a boy of eleven. The boy's mother had gotten word to me through a foundation in New York that he had incurable cancer. It was his fervent desire to meet Vincent Price.

I stood in the wings, watching Vincent on the stage talk to the boy for almost an hour beneath a single work light. They both spoke softly, and the boy's eyes were beaming with excitement when he left while Vincent's were glistening with tears. It was a heartfelt moment that seemed to me the finest Price performance of all.

Ordinarily, a short engagement on Broadway means the end of future productions. It was not to be this time. The Round-About Theater, an established theater company in Manhattan, brought the play back to New York a few months later for a limited engagement. That was so successful, they did it again for another limited engagement. Lo and behold, it didn't stop there.

Several universities and colleges in the country booked him for one night and two night engagements. Many of these institutions have auditoriums and concert halls of several hundred seats. He packed them in. They loved it and he loved it, and he kept on doing it for more than a year. It was not only gratifying artistically for Vincent, but financially for both of us. Eventually, he went on to play it in Canada, Australia, and Hong Kong and finally ended the tour at the Westwood Playhouse in California. It was there that I last saw him in 1982.

A year before he died of lung cancer in 1993, he sent me a despondent note ruminating over the terrible realities of growing old. "I just mourned my

83rd birthday and wish I could shed the last five." His wife, Coral Browne, passed away only a year before. They had such a strong, loving marriage and adored each other. He was too frail to attend her funeral service, but he had the director John Schlesinger read a letter saying that in missing Coral, "I find that I'm missing much of life itself."

There had always been talk of Price being gay but, like Minnelli, I never saw any evidence of it. It was losing Coral, I believe, that brought about and aided his own death. Not just an accomplished actor, but a fine and compassionate man.

CHAPTER 41

At the time of the San Francisco opening of *Diversions and Delights*, something else was happening which seemed to me almost unreal. I had followed the Wilde play with a biographical drama I called *Summer Voices*, a coming of age in the 1930s when I spent two hot summer weeks with my Aunt Sara and Uncle Ferd in Visalia, California, a little agricultural town in the San Joaquin valley. Frank Gilroy loved the play enough to take an option on it and contacted Oliver Hailey, an accomplished playwright himself, who then produced it at the Circle Theater in Hollywood. Opening night came only two days after the opening of *Diversions and Delights* in San Francisco.

Those weeks in my aunt and uncle's old two story clapboard house provided me with a dramatic structure based on my aunt's tormented desire to adopt a baby. Soap operas were just as popular then as they are today, only they were on the radio. The boy in my play fantasizes that a character in one of the soaps, *Ma Perkins*, comes to life, enters the house, and brings utter joy to the family at a time of crisis.

Rehearsals were held for several weeks under Gennaro Montanino, an accomplished and very likable theatrical director. The leads, Marion Mercer and Charles Aidman, had many theatrical credits and we were lucky to get them. Marion reminded me very much of my aunt, the lead character.

The Circle Theater was so small that the surrounding audience could reach out and touch the actors. Not that they ever did, but I found the close proximity distracting. There were only two reviews which were not unusual then for an off-Broadway play in Los Angeles. The *Los Angeles Times* critic found it involving, but bleak and dark. For her, the second act climax with a single moment of possible infanticide overpowered the many comic moments and lighthearted feeling of the play. Variety was fair, but not a review that would bring people to the theater, especially when there was no advertising budget. My feelings remain the same. The cast was ideal and, for me personally, they brought back once again that youthful summer in Visalia.

"GUNFIGHT AT THE WRITERS GUILD CORRAL" The headline of the *L.A. Times* the day after a Writers Guild Board meeting. I was serving on a strike negotiation committee when the Guild was accused of being either too militant or not militant enough by its own members. Tempers got heated into a shouting match. I called out "Point of order!" during the meeting and made a plea for civility. "For God's sake, let's take our anger out on the suits, not each other." The next day, the *Los Angeles Times* printed my earnest plea for unity word for word.

It was the prolonged strike of 1988, however, that was devastating to many writers and their families. When it was over, I was asked to run for president with the thought that I might bring some harmony and camaraderie to the Guild. I knew that I couldn't devote enough time to the position nor did I really have the disposition for it. They asked me then if I would run for vice president. I accepted, campaigned, and won. After all the Guild had done for me, it was the least I could do for the Guild.

SMALL SCREEN

CHAPTER 42

In the world of literature, a collection of different stories is termed an anthology but, in television, they use the acronym, MOW. Movies of the Week. All three major networks carried them for years until cable came along. I was fortunate to have an agent, Bob Graham of CAA, who guided me through his winning ways and sagacity to a friendship that still endures today. With him, I became closely involved in both the fictional and the non-fictional (or docudrama) form for the television screen. Although smaller in size, it often tackled subjects even closer to the tribulations of the human condition.

Rosalie Asher Home - Sacramento

"Lousy Jew Scum, go back to kike land and take the sex fiend with you!"

One of the letters of hate mail that Rosalie Asher showed me from the time she was defending Caryl Chessman on death row. He was called the "Red-Light Bandit", a man who stalked unsuspecting female drivers in lonely areas, flashing a light through red cellophane tape on his car to appear like a police car. He would then take his victim to another area and sexually abuse her. A petty-ante thief, cocky and snide, Chessman claimed he had nothing to do with it. "I'm no lousy pervert attacking women for five bucks! I get all the women I want!" Under the Lindbergh kidnapping law at the time, a guilty verdict could mean the death chamber even if no murder was committed. There was only circumstantial evidence, but the court found him guilty.

Thus began twelve years on death row at San Quentin with eight stays of execution. The case then became a cause célèbre throughout the world. Albert Schweitzer, Aldous Huxley, and Pablo Casals were among those who condemned the execution. One stay of execution was granted because President Eisenhower was about to visit Uruguay and didn't want to face any pro-Chessman demonstrations. Chessman (an IQ of 160) wrote several best-selling books in prison, proclaiming his innocence and criticizing capital punishment. His execution took place in 1960.

Living in California, I knew much of this from the news. I was always intrigued by the case and began by going over the numerous and voluminous court transcripts. I read all of Chessman's books before interviewing his lawyer, Rosalie Asher, in Sacramento. Through all the years he was on death row, she continuously appealed his conviction and kept a large collection of trial transcripts and newspaper stories about Chessman. The more I researched the project and discussed it with her, the more I became convinced that Chessman was not the "Red Light Bandit". He may have pulled off some robberies, but rape and kidnapping didn't seem to be his milieu. It amused me that Chessman had felt the charge was beneath him. "After all," he said, "I've got my standards."

In Asher's last appeal to the court, she used transcripts to indicate a breach of judicial conduct and, in addition, claimed that twelve years on death row constituted cruel and unusual punishment. On the day of Chessman's execution, she met with Judge Goodman, the Chief Justice of the California Supreme Court. It was Asher's final appeal. To her deep gratification, Judge Goodman finally gave Chessman a stay of execution that would keep him permanently free of a death penalty. He immediately had his secretary make a call to inform them and stop the execution. At that very moment, however, Chessman was being escorted to the gas chamber. The secretary dialed the wrong number. By the time the call finally came through to the warden, it was too late. Chessman had already been strapped in the chair. The execution could not be stopped. It sounds like fiction, but it actually happened.

Ms. Asher showed me the San Francisco paper verifying the incident and I made it a part of my script. Later, an article by Mark Harris in the *TV Guide*,

"Unmasking the Docudrama", stated that Docudramas were mostly fiction and claimed that I had made up the phone call to the warden. I wrote the *TV Guide* editor, hoping they would print my evidence of the incident. They referred me to the author, Harris. I gave him the facts, but he continued to stick to his claim which infuriated me. Two months later, I got my revenge.

Mark Harris was one of the participants invited to a symposium in Ojai, California, about the responsibility of writing television docudramas. In attendance were many writers, directors, producers, and editors, including the editor of *TV Guide,* all seated facing each other around a huge conference table. I challenged Harris before the group about his responsibility in checking the facts. He had to admit he hadn't verified anything and made a false assumption. He apologized. I then turned to the editor of *TV Guide* and asked him why he didn't publish my response. He said he certainly would next time. Next time?

A chapter title in one of Chessman's books was called *Kill Me If You Can,* and I used it for the Docudrama. Alan Alda was cast as Chessman and, using makeup such as an altered nose and facial features, not only acted the part to perfection, he looked the part. My good friend from *Playhouse 90* days, Buzz Kulick, directed with skillful sensitivity.

NBC slotted it on their schedule as "The Big Event". The press across the country gave it good reviews with John O'Connor of *The New York Times* adding that "Alan Alda is quite simply brilliant as Chessman." A humorous, somewhat less than respectful review came from the *New York News*. Referring to Alda's character in *M*A*S*H,* the headline read, "Hawkeye Gets the Chair!" My favorite comment came in a letter by Rosalie Asher expressing her deep appreciation for my screenplay and hoping our paths might cross again.

Tammy Wynette Home - Nashville

Tammy, queen of country western stars, was appearing at the Grand Old Opry with other great country western singers for a benefit to support the Nashville Fire Department. I was writing a television movie of her life based on her book, *Stand By Your Man* (even though she had been married five times). It was also the title of her most popular song.

A television station crew was in her house for a promotion to publicize a new song she had just recorded with her fourth husband, the country western star, George Jones. He had given Tammy a tremendous start in her career but after they were married, subjected her to physical abuse through his frequent alcoholic binges. That was long ago, he was in recovery, and they were good friends now.

When he arrived at the house, Tammy implored him to perform that night for the benefit. He said he hadn't appeared in public since his recovery and begged off. Tammy asked me if I'd like to see the show. I told her I'd love to see it if I could watch from backstage to get the full experience. I didn't expect, however, what happened that night.

The Grand Old Opry House was now in a new structure a few miles out of town. I was escorted directly to the dressing room areas, and the first person I saw coming in was Johnny Cash who arrived with his wife, both in full length mink coats. In contrast, another western star, Waylon Jennings, looked as though he had just come from a cattle roundup.

Tammy took me to a place in the wings where I could see the show and pointed out that she would be the second one on the bill. I was standing there, waiting for her to begin her first number when, to my surprise, George Jones appeared at my side. He did show up. We were both watching Tammy on stage when Johnny Cash approached and stood next to us. At that moment, Tammy told the audience she had a wonderful treat for them. "If I'm not mistaken, I swear I can see George Jones in the wings. Maybe, if we encourage him, he might come out and sing with me!" With that announcement, the audience went wild. They not only applauded, they stood up and a few of them even stamped their feet. "Come on, George!" she said. "They want you! Ladies and gentlemen, right here is the greatest country western singer in the world!"

I glanced at Johnny Cash. He seemed more than a little disturbed by Tammy's announcement. Jones went out on the stage to join her. Together now, they sang a duet to thunderous applause as Johnny Cash turned away.

It was a memorable moment for me, no matter how the project turned out.

The next morning, with no interruptions (and no Sinatra hesitancy), Tammy spoke about her several husbands. I asked her about an incident in her book where she stated that her second husband took pictures of her as she stepped out of the bathtub. Just a snapshot. She thought nothing of it. But a few months later, when she was appearing at a club, a man came up to her and showed her a picture in a girlie magazine. The same photo he took of her stepping out of the tub. Her husband had sold the picture. I asked her if she was absolutely certain this happened, as it could be considered libelous. She swore to me it was true. Every word of it.

I incorporated it into my screenplay, but when my script was submitted to the network legal department for approval, they said I would have to delete the incident as the second husband was already suing Tammy for defamation. The CBS legal department wanted no part of that. I was forced to eliminate the second husband.

Annette O'Toole played Tammy. Since she started her own career as a singer, her voice was used for the musical numbers to impressive effect. My daughter, Jennifer, played a small part in the production appearing as a call girl in a confrontation with Tammy. She pulled it off so well, a father could worry.

The Stanford University Medical Center

A team of doctors and nurses wearing full scrubs stand over a patient at the Stanford University Medical Center as I look on, observing an operation for a docudrama about a heart attack victim desperately in need of a heart transplant. The lead surgeon, wearing a red bandana, was smiling beneath his mask and others joined in. They were soon laughing, and I couldn't wait to find out what had happened. That afternoon, I was told that open heart surgery can go on for many hours with accompanying tension. The tension, itself, can become detrimental. A momentary break of any kind is welcomed and altogether beneficial. I thought it was unusual enough to use for my script, *Transplant*, but then I decided it would divert attention from the story and doubted that people would believe it.

Before I left the hospital, while we were moving through the lounge, the surgeon pointed out two men, seated in wheelchairs, who had gone through heart transplants. One of them was actually smoking! The surgeon said the hospital had no authority to control the will of a patient.

Tone, the critic for *Variety,* said that I created "...lovable and credible characters throughout." I didn't. The heart victim and his wife I wrote about were drawn from life and lived successfully through the arduous ordeal. I hoped I had done them justice.

Roger Gimble Productions - Hollywood

It's two weeks before filming starts on a three hour production of *The Amazing Howard Hughes.* I've researched every aspect of Hughes' life, his exploits in aviation and as a motion picture producer. Who would be our Howard Hughes? One young man, among others, walked in and looked the part. In fact, the resemblance was startling. But could he act? We told him a few facts about Hughes, specifically his Texas upbringing, and asked him if he could manage a Texas accent. His reply was not easily forgotten. "Which part of Texas?"

As it turned out, Tommy Lee Jones, almost unknown then, had once worked in the Texas oil fields. He could handle any Texas accent. He read a scene for us and was hired immediately. It was a lucky break for the production. In fact, the entire cast couldn't have been better. Some critics remarked that I didn't really capture the strange, mysterious, elusive quality of Howard Hughes. Right. No other writer has either.

Rosemont Productions - Hollywood

"Is this shit any good?"

Norman Rosemont was asking me about my first draft of an adaptation of *The Red Badge of Courage* for television.

"Brilliant," I told him. Of course, the novel by Stephen Crane was a Civil War masterpiece, amazing given the man who wrote it wasn't born until after the Civil War. I treated it with reverence, letting the personal story of a young man facing death be the key. It was sent to the studio heads who wanted to know if I could weave in a love story. I refused. Norman pointed out that there was a mention in the book of the boy leaving behind a childhood girlfriend. I wrote in a fleeting visual glimpse of her, shown in flashback, thus keeping the integrity of the book. It received excellent notices with Cecil Smith of the Los Angeles Times calling it, "An immensely stirring experience."

I was working on *The Hunchback of Notre Dame*, starring Anthony Hopkins, when Norman asked the question once again, "Is this shit any good?"

"Brilliant." I told him. By now, Norman was sometimes called "Stormin' Norman". He had a plaque in front of his London production office in gold script, "To err is human. To forgive is not Rosemont policy." Directors never liked him, but for me, a writer's dream. He refused to let anyone make line changes unless they were cleared with me first. This directive of his continued for *Les Miserables, Ivanhoe, and The Tale of Two Cities*. It meant several long-distance calls from Europe during filming to see if I'd approve an additional line or a cut from a speech. Oh, yes, I did like Norman.

San Francisco Clinic

Dr. Don Francis, the man who had eradicated smallpox in many places around the world, was furious. His anger was directed at President Reagan for doing nothing about AIDS during the whole time he was President. Francis told me this, predicting that AIDS could decimate populations everywhere. It was 1988, and I was on assignment to adapt a book by Randy Shilts called *The Band Played On* which focused on four men who were losing their partners to a mysterious disease.

I later interviewed several of these men and one spoke movingly of their plight, the fear of the unknown disease, the wrenching fevers, the wasting away of their lives. As he continued, he hesitated for a long moment. I waited. He was in tears.

With the strong approval of Mr. Shilts, I turned in my script to NBC. Word came that it was too complicated. Make it more of a medical story. More doctors. Less gays. Without being specific, there was no question they wanted me to reduce or eliminate the plight of gay men in San Francisco and New York, a controversial subject. Their plight for me was the very heart of the story. Conferences became contentious and numerous. I didn't hear anything for a month. When another month went by, I started another project.

The Band Played On was eventually made. HBO took it over from NBC with another writer and it did become a medical story with Alan Alda playing Dr. Robert Gallo. A *Los Angeles Times* reporter called to ask me why NBC hadn't produced my script. Her angle, I believe, was to have me say that NBC didn't have the guts to go into the lives of gay men in a sympathetic way. I did believe it, but I couldn't prove it and I didn't respond to the allegation.

Unfortunately, I never got a chance to speak to Randy Shilts about the HBO production. He died of AIDS in 1990. I had no idea that he had it. Randy Shilts, to me, was one of the most courageous men I ever met. The waste of his life and others cut so short.

Home of Joe McGinniss – Williamstown, Mass.
"I hear that you're an expert in the writing of triple homicides."

Jeffrey MacDonald, a Green Beret doctor, surprised Joe McGuiness with this off-handed remark when he asked him to write a book about his wife and children's murder, a book to prove his innocence. I met Joe, a brilliant and highly successful journalist, at his home in Williamstown where he told me he thought the remark somewhat unfeeling. Joe started his own investigation but did not reach the conclusion MacDonald wanted. The unexpected result portrayed a complex and fascinating study of a man who appeared to be a loving husband, a devoted father, and…a psychopathic killer. The more people Joe met in his research, the more convinced he became of MacDonald's guilt. Later, the trial confirmed Joe's research. Guilty.

In a quest to find answers to questions that would affect me as a dramatist, I wanted every scene to reflect that the facts in the book were correct. I was determined to meet everyone involved in the murder case, starting with the two trial attorneys who confirmed Joe's reporting and added a few story elements of their own. My most important visit was meeting the Kassabs, the victim's mother and stepfather, in New York. It was Freddy Kassab who initially believed in his son-in-law's innocence until he discovered otherwise and became determined to bring him to justice. They were more than anxious to answer all of my questions.

Interviewing someone for the purpose of writing a book is different in many ways than that of writing a screenplay. In one incident, for instance, when Jeff visited the Kassabs after the murders, I wanted visual details along with the facts. How was he dressed? Did you serve him lunch? Did he stay long? What was his attitude? Mildred was helpful, but Freddy was still filled with rage against MacDonald and bitterly disappointed over the verdict of the trial. A lifetime sentence with a possibility of parole wasn't good enough for Freddy. He wanted him executed.

My outline-treatment took a good deal longer because of so much additional research. The producers got impatient. Screenwriters have a saying. "Do you want it good or do you want it tomorrow?" I swear sometimes they'd rather have it tomorrow. I took my time.

Two more trips to visit Joe were necessary before I began the screenplay. He was enormously helpful. I obtained all of the trial transcripts of the courtroom testimony, numbering hundreds of pages which I spread out on the dining room table. Bobbie and I had to eat dinner in the kitchen for six weeks. The courtroom dialogue that I used came directly from those transcripts. I had many other documents, letters, newspaper articles, and statements made by participants.

I found myself so caught up with the lives of Jeff MacDonald's wife and his two little children that I couldn't shake it off from day to day. I was convinced now, as Joe had been, that MacDonald had brutally murdered his family. I wanted there to be no question that the facts were correct. One of the producers asked me to fictionalize some scenes which he thought would make the story more dramatic. I convinced him that nothing could be more dramatic than the true story itself. Any fiction would taint the entire project.

Casting was no problem with the exception of an actor to play Freddy. I wanted Karl Malden. This esteemed actor had performed in theater and film with all of the finest actors of our time. I could see him in the part when I was writing it. NBC had their list of actors to play Freddy and I was invited to the casting session. The director, David Greene, resisted casting Malden. I couldn't believe it. I kept hammering away at the producers and David finally gave in. There was no difficulty at all, however, in casting the lovely and luminous actress, Eva Marie Saint, for Malden's wife. Script changes were agreed upon as long as any changes were based on fact. With production underway, I was beginning to think we really had something special.

A screening was held at the Motion Picture Academy with an invited audience of production staff and industry executives. Freddy and Mildred were both present and, more than anything, I wanted their approval. It came, I'm happy to say, in the lobby after the screening.

There was one hell of a lot of publicity about it before it went on the air. MacDonald tried to stop NBC from broadcasting it. In spite of the jury verdict, he still claimed his innocence from his cell and said that the television showing would prejudice his pending appeal for a new federal court trial. NBC stood on firm legal grounds and proceeded with the broadcast which was aired on two evenings. The reviews were all that a writer could hope for. Among them, "Sheer Thriller", "Haunting", "A stunner of a docudrama." As I knew he would, Karl Malden turned in a touching sensitive performance. For two consecutive evenings, *Fatal Vision* came in number one. In fact, it was the highest miniseries for the season or the previous season or any season that I've experienced.

There is an aftermath to this production. A year or so after the telecast, MacDonald, in jail, sued McGinniss for deceiving him by pretending to believe in his innocence, then writing a book that found him guilty. Joe, of course, never promised him anything except the truth. A reputable *Wall Street Journal* critic and journalist, Joe Morgenstern, called the lawsuit "Lunacy at its full height." It came to court, however, and the jury was unable to decide if

McGinniss deceived MacDonald or not, showing no understanding of writers in their quest to be truthful.

I testified at the trial in Los Angeles and faced MacDonald across the courtroom. Knowing what I did from the trial transcripts, what I thought he was capable of, gave me a chill. Journalists spoke up for Joe, including William F. Buckley, noted television, magazine, and newspaper reporter, who said, "It would destroy the profession if the subject was allowed to dictate the contents of books about them. Freedom of speech would simply evaporate." But Joe's publishing company didn't want to get into a protracted law suit and settled out of court, much to Joe's dismay.

Joe Morgenstern put it best when he wrote, "What's the truth about Jeffrey MacDonald? Is he the innocent victim he claims? Hell, no. He's a murderer. A liar and a vicious murderer who killed his pregnant wife and their two daughters. That's what a jury decided in 1979 and that's how McGinniss portrayed him in his book." I couldn't agree more.

A final note about Freddy Kassab. He swore to me, "If MacDonald is ever released from prison, I'll kill the bastard myself!" But that will never come to pass. Jeff MacDonald remains in a federal prison today serving three concurrent life sentences, parole denied. Freddy Kassab has passed away.

Irwin Allen Production Office – 20th Century Fox

"Was this a joke? A script by numbers?" I thought, as I listened to three story editors admonish me for my scene progression in The *Adventures of A Queen*. I did not have the Irwin Allen formula for success. Although I <u>did</u> have comedy, action, and drama, they said I had placed them in a haphazard order. I was puzzled. Haphazard? They informed me, "You've written: drama, drama, comedy, action, action, drama, action. Your scenes aren't in the proper order. They should be drama, action, comedy. Drama, action, comedy, in just that sequence."

But not to worry. They would put it in the Irwin Allen order. And to my embarrassment, they did. It was awful. But don't take my word for it. Reviews confirmed it.

Ballet Class - Lincoln Center, New York
"It's him! It's Villella!"

Edward Villella escorts me into a room full of young ballet dancers for my research about his life as a leading dancer of the New York City Ballet. We had already driven through the tough Brooklyn neighborhood where he grew up and now, he wanted me to see an actual ballet class. From the reaction of the students when they saw Villella, one would think I had walked in with Robert Redford or Paul Newman. You could hear the whispers.

While there, we ran into Rudolph Nureyev who embraced him. "Hello, beautiful Eddy! You are always so beautiful."

Villella was a straight, masculine dancer and some critics said he brought "balls to ballet". Maybe if I had used that as the title for my script, the networks would have given it a green light. Their reason for turning it down? A ballet story wouldn't have enough popular appeal.

Filming in Mississippi
"So you're the little woman who wrote the book that started this big war."

A line spoken by Abraham Lincoln when he was introduced to Harriet Beecher Stowe, the author of *Uncle Tom's Cabin*. The name, Uncle Tom, then became a pejorative for a fawning servant. I was assigned not only to dramatize the story but to set the record straight. Those who actually read the book will find him a heroic figure whose spiritual strength dominates the story. A man of God, of principal, much like Martin Luther King. As a matter of fact, in the closing chapter when Tom is tied, bound to a post and whipped, there is an obvious likening to Christ on the cross.

The summertime filming in Natchez with stars Avery Brooks and Phylicia Rashad was going smoothly until it came to staging a familiar scene of the book in a totally different setting. How could Eliza cross the river on ice floes in August? Impossible! Creating fake ice floes would look just like...fake ice floes. In this production, Eliza, to my embarrassment, crossed the river on a raft. However, I was delighted to find that the critics felt I had dispelled the conventional wisdom and it was, "A different Uncle Tom that should be seen."

Screening room - Hollywood

"Samp-sin! Samp-sin! Come on ova heah!"

On the screen, a young Samson leaves his home to meet Delilah. My script, *Samson and Delilah,* came from several biblical versions and I was seeing the result for the first time. Samson's friend waves to him from across the river and calls out, "Samp-sin!" again.

I rose up, "Stop the film. Hold it! Did you hear what he said? Samp-sin!" I repeated it with the Brooklyn accent. The producer couldn't tell the difference. A few lines were looped later, but most of his dialogue remained mired in Brooklyn ESE. The reviews were not kind. They didn't like the production. They didn't like the script. I completely agree with both opinions.

Kirk Douglas Home – Beverly Hills

"Inherit the Wind. What the hell does that mean?"

I told Kirk, "It comes from the Book of Proverbs, 'He that troubleth his own house shall inherit the wind.' The wind, meaning tribulation." I also reminded him that it had been a famous Pulitzer Prize play, not to mention a feature film. It would be unwise at this point to change the title. Fortunately, my second explanation convinced him to leave it alone.

Inherit the Wind is a fictional dramatization of the famous Scopes monkey trial where a Tennessee schoolteacher was charged with illegally teaching Darwin's theory of evolution. Douglas and his son, Peter, wanted to produce it as a television special. I was chosen to write the adaptation in spite of the fact, as I told them, that the playwrights, Jerry Lawrence and Robert E. Lee, were certainly capable of adapting it themselves. I called Jerry to inform him of the TV production, and he made it clear that he and Bob were disappointed in the earlier motion picture made of it with Spencer Tracey and Fredrick March. I assured him I'd stay as closely as possible to their play.

At our first meeting, Douglas made it made it clear that he had produced many motion pictures and knew his way around screenplays. For a star of his stature, I thought the statement rather gratuitous.

Gregory Peck was signed to play opposite Kirk and, in my visit to Peck's Bel Air home, I found him much more enthusiastic than Kurt about the project. He loved *Inherit the Wind* as a play, but knew there were time restraints on television and worried about the television adaptation. By acting out several scenes together with Peck, we agreed on what to keep, what to omit, and what to expand. I could see that he would be marvelous in the part.

I soon found myself going back and forth between the two men at their homes in separate story consultations. It reminded me of the time I spent with Minnelli and Blaustein in Paris going up and down an elevator of the Georges V for discussions when they weren't speaking to each other. Back and forth over changes that came mostly from Douglas. Peck increasingly resisted the changes that Douglas wanted. I sympathized with Peck and favored his point of view for the most part. Little progress was being made between them in spite of my effort.

Then Kirk laid down the gauntlet. He led me to believe that if Peck complained about any future changes, either Peck would be out or he would be out. He added that Peck wasn't getting that much work these days, anyway. Peck pulled out. I felt he had had enough of Douglas. I wrote Peck a letter expressing my keen disappointment and he wrote back to say he was sorry he couldn't continue, adding, "Let us get together on another project before it's too late."

It wasn't long before Jason Robards was signed on to replace Peck. There couldn't have been a better replacement. He did, in fact, win an Emmy in the part. I personally think Peck would have won the award, too. It's one hell of a part. I attribute to Lawrence and Lee the fact that all reviews were positive. A review that gave me a kick was, "Hoo boy, have we got a TV movie for you!" from

Mark Schwed of the *Los Angeles Herald Examiner*. But the best review came from the two playwrights, Lawrence and Lee, who called to tell me, "You were far more faithful to our play than to the earlier motion picture." I'm sure it'll be produced many more times on stage, television, and theatrical screens.

Rehearsal room – Vancouver, Canada

"Why don't you wait, Mr. Gay, until <u>after</u> the reading, before you decide whether you're so delighted I'm doing the part?"

Bette Davis would have nothing to do with my gratitude for her decision to play the lead in my television drama, *A Piano For Mrs. Cimino,* to be directed by George Schaefer. It was the part of an aging woman, temporarily in a mental breakdown over her husband's death. I was finally getting the chance to meet Betty Davis and work with her.

During the reading, the actors had their scripts in hand as they read. All except Davis. She knew the lines by heart. And she knew that the actors were intimidated by it. "Can we stop for a moment? Some of you might be looking at me unkindly. Consider. Please. It's true that I've already memorized my part at the first reading. I'm not trying to show off. At my age, I must know the lines in advance or I'd never have them."

At the same reading, she also informed the cast she was pleased to see that Mr. Gay did not instruct the actors how the dialogue should be spoken. "Notice he doesn't insert (grimly) or (smiling) or (in tears). Mr. Gay leaves it to <u>us.</u> To the actors. As well he should."

After playing so many parts in summer stock, I had always resented a script instructing me <u>how</u> to say a line. How gratifying to know that Bette Davis felt the same way.

The reaction to *A Piano for Mrs. Cimino* from Daniel Henning in The *Wall Street Journal,* "Hollywood traditionally gives authors two things for writing junk – lots of money and lots of self-contempt.....Mrs. Cimino is the kind of honest work that can keep the TV community from sinking into creative senility."

Women In Film gave Betty Davis a dinner afterward which Bobbie and I attended at the Beverly Wilshire Hotel. We were thrilled to see this celebrated lady of American film up on the dais commanding everyone's attention, still full of life, grit, and self determination. My best review came from Davis herself. "A script of the kind I used to beg Warner Brothers to let me do."

McGinniss home - Williamstown

With author Joe McGinniss again and the story of a picture-perfect father of a picture-perfect family in Tom's River, New Jersey. Not so perfect was the fact that the father was serving a sentence on death row for hiring someone to murder his wife for a large insurance policy. The very heart of the drama, however, was the eventual disillusionment of his two sons who had devoutly believed in their father's innocence, giving birth to the title, *Blind Faith*. In doing my own research, it was important that I once again get the facts from the people involved and get them right.

One of the sons refused to grant me an interview, but the other one, Robbie Marshall, cooperated fully. In fact, he agreed to help us in the production of the film. A painful moment in the script comes when the son visits his father in prison. I saw the filming of it with the actual son standing next to me watching the actors. I couldn't help but wonder what his feelings were. He showed no emotion.

Paul Wendkos was signed to direct and Robert Uric headed a strong cast. *Blind Faith* became the highest rated miniseries of that season. The paperback edition hit the #1 non-fiction best seller on the New York Times list. The *Hollywood Reporter* gave it a backhanded compliment, "There's no excuse for exploiting this tabloid style tragedy. But if you're going to do it, you might as well do it right. And they sure did. ...By turns brilliantly sarcastic, self-demeaning, and heart-rending."

In spite of the success of *Fatal Vision and Blind Faith*, Joe McGinnis swore off writing any more true crime dramas. Then, a lawyer Joe knew told him about a woman, Bonnie Von Stein, whose son, Chris, along with two of his friends, were convicted of murdering her husband. Bonnie then took it upon herself to contact Joe with the hope that a further investigation might shed some additional light on the murder. Chris was proven to be part of the murder scheme, but not at the actual crime, and Bonnie still couldn't believe he was involved. What Joe discovered was of no help to Bonnie except his sympathy and the writing of his book, *Cruel Doubt*. I felt meeting her personally might help me to a better understanding of the crime.

After a cordial greeting, she spoke once again of doubt about Chris' participation. So quiet, so controlled was Bonnie that I had to keep reminding myself we were talking about a very brutal murder in which she, herself, lay in a pool of blood before the police arrived. It may have been a quiet interview but, to me, her calm discussion of it made it very <u>dis</u>quieting. Perhaps she had been through so much that she pushed it away to a space where she wouldn't be hurt anymore.

My next stop was the Yadkinville Correctional Institution in Washington, North Carolina, where Chris was being held on the murder conviction. Entering the detention room, I was surprised to see a very young man with an angelic face seated at a desk. No swaggering bully here, no sullen bratty kid, no cold killer. I attempted to ask probing questions, but his answers were almost as though he was talking about someone else. He still didn't seem to realize the enormity of his crime.

On this particular day, he had just heard that he was being transferred to another prison far away which would mean a five hour drive for Bonnie. He asked me if I could do something to prevent the transfer. I said I'd try and later contacted McGinniss who told me nothing could be done. My visit left me disturbed. I had entered the prison expecting a monster and left it having encountered a lost soul.

There was still one interview to make and it turned a little nasty. Officials at the police station in the town of Washington, North Carolina, had conducted the murder investigation and could furnish a complete account of the arrest. I was in the midst of talking to two of the investigators when the Chief of Police suddenly barged in and turned on me. "You! Get out!"

I tried to explain that NBC had arranged the interview with the two detectives who… "Leave! Now!"

There was nothing else for me to do but go. The incident gives you some idea of how police chiefs trust docudrama writers. I was trying to get everything right, to make it factual, and he wanted no part of it. Fortunately, I was able to visit the county court of records later that day and found most of the information that I had wanted from the police.

Bonnie Von Stein was played by Blythe Danner, one of our best American actresses. Her daughter, Gwyneth Paltrow, unknown then, was hired before her mother for the part of the daughter in the script. *Cruel Doubt* appeared as a four hour miniseries on NBC and topped the ratings. And I will never forget the day I was kicked out of the Washington Police Station.

I was to adapt one more book by Joe McGinniss. The production never came about because, I believe, of the subject, Senator Edward M. Kennedy. Joe wanted interviews with him but was denied. He spent a year on research, in spite of those denials, speaking to everyone who knew him.

The Last Brother was published by Simon and Schuster, and the rights to film the story went to NBC. A firestorm of criticism erupted over a difference between part classic reportage and freeform journalism. A huge campaign began to demean the book as a vindictive diatribe against Kennedy. *Time* magazine and *New York* magazine critics were both negative. Joe fought the charges in several appearances, including a spot on the Larry King show, but NBC got cold feet and bowed out of the miniseries. It was a terrible unfair blow to a magnificent journalist. It was also a great disappointment to me.

House in Paris Suburbs

"Silence!"

Adolph Hitler paces back and forth on a veranda. He looks to be in a triumphant mood with his stride, the movement of his entire body. From a window above, I could swear it was Hitler even though I knew better. It was the production of a CBS three hour television special, *The Bunker,* based upon a book by James O'Donnell about the last days of Hitler. From the very first day I saw Anthony Hopkins in makeup as Hitler, I was astonished.

George Schaefer had been signed to direct and insisted upon two weeks of rehearsal first in London before filming began in Paris. Hopkins and I shared a ride to the London rehearsal studio each morning, and I found him genial, unassuming, and absolutely charming. To see him in rehearsal was a revelation. He'd go over a given scene several times trying out different approaches until he felt it was right. I asked him about his approach to acting and he said he always concentrated the outward physical aspects of a character first. It was similar to Lawrence Olivier with whom he had worked at the Royal Shakespeare Company.

I'd heard he once auditioned for Olivier to join the Company. The scene Hopkins chose was from *Richard III,* the same part that was an acknowledged Olivier triumph on stage. When the audition was over, Hopkins waited for the verdict. There was only silence. According to the report, Olivier finally said, "I see. Richard III. Well. That was a bit cheeky, wasn't it?" I discovered later that, although Hopkins worked for years in the British theater, he never felt comfortable working in London. He was a Welshman and, to him, many British actors were too damned full of themselves.

The reviews of Hopkins' performance confirmed my own opinion. From *Variety,* "Hopkins is first rate, dead-eyed and terrifying." And more to the point, a confirming review from a critic in California. "A performance so skillful that at times you have to remind yourself that you are not watching the real Hitler."

The only sour note came from Howard Rosenberg of the *L.A. Times* who thought Hopkins appeared too "human" in the part of Hitler. This observation, however, was refuted by another critic, Vern Perry, who said, "If we truly want to learn how such horrible things could have happened, and prevent them in the future, we have to understand they were committed by human beings."

London Hotel

There's something about a first reading of a script that's revelatory for everyone. The actors gather for the first time and explore not only their own parts but the play itself. I've never been to a more illustrious gathering of actors than the one that Rosemont drew to the mezzanine room of a West End hotel in London. The script was for the television adaptation of *Witness for the Prosecution* from the Agatha Christie play and the Wilder, Kurnitz filmplay. English actors render a spirited reading even at the first get-together while some American actors tend to mumble through the lines until they can get 'into' a part. God forbid they give a performance at the first reading. We were fortunate as great English actors were available in London for most projects because it allowed them to work on a film during the day and still play on stage at night.

Heading the cast was Sir Ralph Richardson, considered by many to be one of the ten greatest actors in the English speaking world. I felt privileged just to be there. Deborah Kerr, whom I hadn't seen since *Separate Tables* in 1957, looked just as attractive. Wendy Hiller, who captured an Academy Award for *Separate Tables,* sat next to Donald Pleasence whom I remembered from *Soldier Blue.* And next to him was Diana Rigg, a well-known British actress of stage and film. I was a bit worried about Beau Bridges in this company, but he proved adept in his part from the very beginning.

In a restaurant near the Old Bailey courtroom, I watched as the entire restaurant staff treated Sir Ralph as if he were the prime minister of England, a reverence not paid to many actors. After lunch, Norman asked me to drive over to the costumers in Sir Ralph's limousine. I jumped at the chance.

The two of us sat in the back seat where I looked forward to a one on one chat. Sir Ralph, however, was only interested in one subject. He wanted an automated chairlift for one of his scenes, a stairway device that would allow the camera to follow him up to the second floor, just as Charles Loughton used in the previous filming of *Witness for the Prosecution.* I explained that the location Norman chose had a regular elevator, no chair lift. Sir Ralph became very agitated. "My dear boy, I simply must have a chair lift, you see. It's so much more cinematic. This is not something that I tell you lightly. You're the writer. Now, do speak to this Rosemont fellow about it and see what you can do."

I told him there really wasn't much of a chance that Rosemont would install one. Not with an elevator already in place.

He pleaded with me. "You must tell him, you must." I found myself in the uncomfortable position of turning down Sir Ralph Richardson. I did speak to Norman and gave it an earnest try. The result was no surprise to me. One of our greatest actors didn't get his chair lift. Norman's response was, "Screw him."

The filming was done at Twikenham Studios in London, and I felt from the beginning this production was going to be a good one. I wasn't disappointed. *The New York Times:* "Television would have to come up with a very special package to justify another version of this mystery thriller. It has." Sir Ralph garnered similar kudos but, alas, he never got his chair lift.

CURTAIN CALL

CHAPTER 43

Another great British actor came into my life in the person of Donald Sinden. And, this time, on the stage. My first agent in California, Swannie, with the lapel carnations and the pin striped suits, had passed on, but his assistant, Ben Kamsler, had always loved my Wilde play. Without my knowledge, he contacted a producer in London, Patricia McNaughton, and sent her the script. She didn't know Ben and didn't even bother to read it for a month or so, but when she did, she saw it as a part for Sinden, one of the major stars of the British theater. Negotiations were made, and she was delighted to tell me that a premiere limited engagement was scheduled to be held at the Princess Grace Theater in Monte Carlo.

Arriving in Monte Carlo, Bobbie and I found the Princess Grace Theater where a large poster displayed Donald Sinden, in costume, as Oscar Wilde. I had seen so many posters before with Vincent Price as Wilde that it seemed a little strange.

That night, we met Patricia McNaughton in the lobby of the theater just before curtain of the first preview performance. She told us that Sinden didn't know we had planned to come. I was keyed up with anticipation. How would Sinden compare with Price?

Strolling on stage, just as Price did, Sinden offered a different looking figure of Wilde. He was robust and stockier, his manner less flamboyant and his costume copied directly from an authentic photo. It was his first time before an audience as Wilde and he seemed a bit nervous. As the night went on, I found Sinden somewhat less effective in the lighter comedic moments than Price. He was more effective, however, in the darker scenes of the second act. At the final curtain, the applause was loud and sustained.

After the play, Patricia introduced me and Bobbie to Sinden and his wife in the dressing room, as well as the director Frank Dunlop. They were all genuinely surprised that we flew in from California for the opening and invited us to dinner with them at a nearby restaurant. Dunlop wanted to know my reaction to Sinden's performance. I told him, diplomatically, that I was impressed, but Dunlop wanted particulars. I said that since this was Sinden's first public performance, he couldn't know as yet where the laughter would be, a situation which could throw off one's timing. I quickly added that he'd soon grow used to an audience and make adjustments. Dunlop was adamant. "I want your honest opinion of Sinden!" I repeated that there were comic areas in the first act which could be realized more fully in time. Dunlop became defensive. "Don't you realize Donald Sinden is the greatest comedic actor in the British theater today?" I immediately acknowledged it and wondered how the hell I got into this bickering over what I thought was very mild criticism.

Nothing was spoken of Dunlop's direction as yet, and perhaps that was a key to his annoyance. Actually, it wasn't as effective as Joseph Hardy's direction with Price, but I didn't say that to Dunlop. I was not here to create any problems and I *was* genuinely delighted with what I had seen. I also knew that Sinden would be getting better and better with each performance. Dunlop must have known it, too, but he was too defensive to admit it. As for Donald Sinden himself? Bigger than life and absolutely delightful.

The next night was something very special. In Europe, an author or playwright is king. Bobbie and I were invited, as honored guests, to be seated next to Prince Rainier in the first row of the mezzanine. During the performance, I kept half an eye on the Prince and was relieved to see he was enjoying it. During the intermission, we were escorted to a private room to be introduced to the

Prince. The room was small and filled with cigarette smoke. It was 1988 and everyone smoked...everyone... including the Prince. We chatted through a blue gray haze. Before leaving Monte Carlo the next day, Patricia said she thought she could get a London opening in the spring. And, indeed, she did.

In January of 1990, *Diversions and Delights* opened at the Comedy Playhouse Theatre near Trafalgar Square. Bobbie and I were invited to come to London at our expense. The lobby was full as we made our way downstairs to the lounge for a scan of the audience before the curtain. We couldn't stay there however, due to the thick, eye smarting, lung choking clouds of smoke. Was the entire English population addicted to cigarettes?

Curtain up. I could tell immediately that Sinden seemed more in control of the part. But this was opening night in London and all of the critics were there. He had every right to be a little nervous and, near the end of the first act, nerves did strike in a most unfortunate way. He left out a comedic soliloquy that provides a contrast to the dramatic speech at the end of the first act. Somehow, he just skipped past it. Bobbie and I exchanged a grim glance. Vincent Price had slipped up a line or two on his opening night in San Francisco, but nothing of this importance. The audience couldn't know, of course, that Sinden had omitted it, but I knew and I hoped it wouldn't affect the reaction to the play.

We retreated to the downstairs lounge at intermission to hear any possible comments. We found, however, that everyone in the lounge was immersed in a new wave of smoky impenetrable haze. We skipped the comments.

Soon after the curtain in the second act, Sinden decided to put back the missing soliloquy of the first. It didn't fit. But then...to my surprise, he went on to a poignant performance of the dramatic second act. We left the theater full of hope even though we prepared for the worst.

The telephone awakened us very early in bed the next morning. It was Patricia. "Have you read the papers? Three excellent reviews in the *Express*, the *Mail*, and the *Standard*." She sounded excited and we were wide awake within moments. Then, as in New York, came the assault. A critical, destructive review from *The London Times* and a similar one from *The Observer*. The two papers had, and still have, the same power as *The New York Times*. Even Donald Sinden took a couple hits.

Patricia decided to close after a few weeks run, but soon after, she was able to organize a successful tour throughout Great Britain. I felt a hell of a lot better for Donald Sinden's sake that the experience ended on an up note.

EPILOGUE

What a grand experience to be in the company of actors in the theater once again. It was the influence of two revered actors, Frederick March and Florence Eldridge, who gave me the confidence of starting a career I hadn't planned on. So how did I get caught up in writing? I look at it this way. In any given script, I get to play all of the parts. The whole cast. Every line. Out loud. It's a way for me to tell if it works. The joy of writing has always been in the first draft, just yourself and the characters on the page. A draft that's yours and yours alone. Of course, we have others to bring it to life but it's the writer before anyone else. As we say in the Writers Guild, "Where were you when the page was empty?"

I have to say that, for me, it's an addiction and I have no plans to stop. The play I'm working on now might reach the boards and it might not. But it's the work. It's always the work that counts. Do I miss acting? No. I'm perfectly... No. That is...sometimes, in the dark of night...

In a theater. Just a work light illuminates the stage. I don't know what theater. But I do know that someone's watching me out front. I can't see him. There's a script in my hand. I'm reading for a part. I don't know what part. I don't know what play. It doesn't matter. I'm doing well. I feel good about it. When I finish, there's utter silence. I turn to leave, but a voice in the darkness calls out to me.

"Can you do a harelip?"

ACKNOWLEDGEMENTS

We are eternally grateful to those who supported us through the years this book was written.

To Frank Gilroy who inspired us with his encouragement and advice.

To Elizabeth Ralser, freelance editor and close friend who gave so many hours of her time.

To everyone affiliated with the Santa Barbara Writers Conference, especially director Marcia Meier, instructors Cork Milner and Marla Miller, talented writer and dear friend, Lori Gervasi.

To Paul Fedorko, whose passion for *Run Silent Run Deep* will never be forgotten.

To Ben, for your devotion and endless passion to Hollywood nostalgia; we remain deeply indebted to your efforts on our behalf.

And especially, to our family members: Bobbie, Ron, Julianne, Larry, Marianne, Liz, Dave, Casey, and Hayley. This book is for all of you.

CREDITS

FEATURE FILMS

Run Silent, Run Deep (UA 1958)

Separate Tables (UA 1958) (Shared credit with Terence Rattigan)

The Happy Thieves (UA 1961)

The Four Horsemen of the Apocalypse (MGM 1962) (Shared credit with Robert Ardry)

The Courtship of Eddie's Father (MGM 1963)

The Hallelujah Trail (UA 1965)

The Last Safari (Paramount 1967)

The Power (MGM 1968)

No Way to Treat a Lady (Paramount 1968)

Soldier Blue (AVCO Embassy 1970)

Sometimes a Great Notion (Universal 1971)

Pocket Money (National General Pictures 1972) Adaptation

Hennessy (AIP 1976)

A Matter of Time (AIP 1976)

LIVE TELEVISION
Kraft Television Theatre
Goodyear Playhouse
Playhouse 90
Lux Video Theatre
Armstrong Circle Theatre

FILMS FOR TELEVISION
All My Darling Daughters (ABC 1972)
My Darling Daughters Anniversary (ABC 1973)
The Chadwick Family (ABC 1974)
Things in Their Season (CBS 1974)
The Red Badge of Courage (NBC 1974)
Adventures of the Queen (CBS 1975)
The Amazing Howard Hughes (CBS 1975)
Kill Me If You Can (NBC 1977)
The Court-Martial of George Armstrong Custer (CBS 1977)
Captains Courageous (CBS 1977)
Les Miserables (CBS Hallmark 1978)
Transplant (CBS 1979)
A Private Battle (CBS 1980)
A Tale of Two Cities (CBS 1980)
The Bunker (CBS 1981)
Berlin Tunnel (CBS 1981)
Dial M for Murder (ABC 1981)
Stand By Your Man (CBS 1981)

The Long Summer of George Adams (NBC 1982)

Piano for Mrs. Cimino (CBS 1982)

The Hunchback of Notre Dame (CBS Hallmark 1982)

Ivanhoe (CBS 1982)

Witness for the Prosecution (CBS Hallmark 1982)

Samson and Delilah (ABC 1984)

Fatal Vision (CBS 1984)

Doubletake (CBS 1985)

Manhunt for Claude Dallas (CBS 1985)

Uncle Tom's Cabin (Showtime 1982)

Windmills of the Gods (CBS 1986)

Six Against the Rock (NBC 1987)

Inherit the Wind (NBC 1989)

Around the World in 80 Days (NBC 1989)

Blind Faith (NBC 1990)

Shadow of a Doubt (NBC Hallmark 1991)

Trial (NBC 1991)

Burden of Proof (ABC 1992)

Cruel Doubt (NBC 1992)

Trick of the Eye (ABC 1995)

Summer of Fear (CBS 1996)

THEATER

Christophe Chelsea Theatre Group, N.Y.C. 1965

Diversions and Delights
    Eugene O'Neil Theatre, N.Y.C. 1977

Princess Grace Theater, Monte Carlo 1988
Playhouse Theatre, London 1990
Ruby Theater at the Complex Hollywood 2007
Germinal Stage, Denver, Colorado 2007

Summer Voices Circle Theatre, L.A. 1977

AWARDS

Writers Guild Laurel Award for Television Lifetime Achievement

Academy Award Nomination

Emmy Award Nomination

5 Writers Guild Nominations

Cable/Ace Nomination

Edgar Allen Poe Nomination

Christopher Award

Caucus Honors Award

AGA Media Award

WGA Edmund H. North Award

WGA Morgan Cox Award

INDEX

A Matter of Time
Abie's Irish Rose
Adler, Luther
Adventures of A Queen
Agnew, Spiro
Alda, Alan
Allen, Irwin
Amazing Dunninger Show, The
Amazing Howard Hughes, The
American Academy of Dramatic Arts
American International Pictures
Apartment 3C
Armstrong Circle Theater
Arsenic and Old Lace
Asher, Rosalie
Atom Squad

Band Played On, The
Beecher, Milton
Beery, Wallace
Bergen, Candice
Bergman, Ingrid
Bickford, Charles
Bilshan and the Thief
Blaustein, Julian
Blind Faith
Blithe Spirit

Boothbay Playhouse
Borowsky, Marvin
Boyd, Stephen
Bradbury, Ray
Brando, Marlon
Bridges, Beau
Brodkin, Herb
Browne, Coral
Buckley, Christopher
Bunker, The
Burton, Richard

Carnegie Hall
Cash, Johnny
Chatterton, Ruth
Chelsea Theater Group
Chessman, Caryl
Christophe
Circle Theater
Cobb, Lee J.
Colla, Richard
Comedy Playhouse Theater
Condon, Richard
Courtship of Eddy's Father, The
Cruel Doubt

Davidson, Gordon

Davis, Bette
Day Before Atlanta, The
Dempsey, Jack
Desire Under the Elms
Devil As a Roaring Lion, The
Devil's Disciple, The
Diversions & Delights
Douglas, Kirk
Dunlop, Frank

Eldridge, Florence
Eugene O'Neill Theater

Fatal Vision
Ferry Boat Crisis at Friday Point, The
Fonda, Henry
Forbes, Ralph
Ford, Glenn
Ford Theater
Foreman, John
Four Horsemen of the Apocalypse, The
Francis, Don

Gable, Clark
Gaines, Blanche
Gilroy, Frank
Gimble, Roger
Gish, Lillian
Goldman, William
Goodyear Playhouse
Graham, Robert
Greene, David
Guillerman, John
Gullick, Bill

Hagen, Uta
Hailey, Oliver
Hallelujah Trail, The
Happy Thieves, The
Hardy, Joseph
Harris, Mark
Harrison, Rex
Hart, Dolores

Hathaway, Henry
Hayworth, Rita
Hecht, Harold
Hennessey
Hepburn, Audrey
Hill, George Roy
Hill, James
Hiller, Wendy
Hopkins, Anthony
Houseman, John
How the West Was Won
Hunchback of Notre Dame
Huston, John

Importance of Being Earnest, The
Inherit the Wind

Jaeckel, Richard
Jehlinger, Charles
Jones, George
Jones, Shirley
Jones, Tommy Lee

Kalfin, Robert
Karloff, Boris
Kassab, Fred
Keith, Sherwood
Kennedy, Ted
Kerr, Deborah
Kill Me If You Can
Kraft Television Theater
Kulick, Buzz

Lancaster, Burt
Lansbury, Angela
Last Brother, The
Last Safari, The
Lawrence, Jerry
Lee, Robert E.
Leeds, Phil
Lehman, Ernest
Leigh, Dorian
Levant, Oscar

Index 225

Levy, Frank
Loeb, Philip
Lumet, Sydney
Lux Video Theater

MacDonald, Jeffrey
Mackendrick, Sandy
Maddow, Ben
Malden, Karl
Mann, Delbert
March, Fredric
Marines Memorial Theater
Marlowe, Harvey
Marshall, George
McGinniss, Joe
McNaughton, Patricia
Mercer, Marion
Minnelli, Liza
Minnelli, Vincent
Mirisch, Walter
Monash, Paul
Montanino, Gennaro
Mr. and Mrs. Mystery
Murphy, Audie

Nash, N. Richard
Negro Ensemble
Neighborhood Playhouse School of the Theater
Nelson, Ralph
New Amsterdam Theater
Newman, Paul
Niven, David
No Way to Treat A Lady

O'Brian, Jack
Odets, Clifford
O'Herlihy, Dan
Olivier, Laurence
Ormandy, Eugene
Out of Dust

Paltrow, Gwyneth

Peck, Gregory
Piano for Mrs. Cimino, A
Playhouse 90
Pleasance, Donald
Power, The
Prarie Night
Preston, James
Price, Vincent
Princess Grace Theater
Pollock, Sydney

Rattigan, Terence
Reading Playhouse
Red Badge of Courage
Red Channels
Reed, Mark
Remick, Lee
Richardson, Ralph
Rigg, Diana
Robards, Jason
Robin Hood Theater
Rose of Tibet, The
Rosemont, Norman
Run Silent, Run Deep
Russell, Kurt

Saint, Eva Marie
Sarrazin, Michael
Schaefer, George
Schultz, Randy
Second Best Bed
Sentry, The
Separate Tables
Serling, Rod
Sharp, Don
Siegel, Sol
Sinatra, Frank
Sinden, Donald
Smith, Bernard
Soldier Blue
Sometimes A Great Notion
Stand By Your Man
Steiger, Rod
Stewart, James

Stranger, The
Strauss, Peter
Sturges, John
Summer Voices
Swanson, H. N.
Sweet Smell of Success, The

Taylor, Elizabeth
Taylor, Robert Lewis
Theater Guild
Thulin, Ingrid
Transplant
Travels of Jaimie McPheeters, The

Uncle Tom's Cabin
Unforgiven, The
U.S. Coast Guard

Valente, Renée
Von Stein, Bonnie
Von Stein, Chris
Villella, Edward

Wayne, Frank
Webb, James
Wise, Robert
Wiseman, Joseph
Witness for the Prosecution
Woodward, Joanne
Writers Guild of America, West
Wynette, Tammy

www.ingramcontent.com/pod-product-compliance
Lightning Source LLC
Chambersburg PA
CBHW071433150426
43191CB00008B/1116